THE MOTORCYCLE HEARSE
AND OTHER UNDERTAKINGS

This book is dedicated to Stuart and Milly,
my other published works.

THE MOTORCYCLE HEARSE

and other undertakings

Stories from the life and work of a hospital chaplain —
funny, harrowing, educational, outrageous, spooky,
and true.

Ian Morris

Published by Crossover Communications Limited,
Reading

First published in 2006 in Great Britain by
Crossover Communications Limited
www.xover.co.uk
ISBN-13: 978-0-9553811-0-2
ISBN-10: 0-9553811-0-X

Copyright © Ian Morris 2006

Cover by Julia Robinson

Printed by The Burlington Press

Contents

Acknowledgements

I am indebted above all to the many people whose honesty, openness, courage, and humour constitute the raw material of this book.

There are of course no real experts on the subject of death, for one very obvious reason: they are all dead. But before they died they shared with me their insights into their experience of dying, or rather of living with a life-limiting condition. Some I was able to thank at the time. To the others I hope that the existence of this work constitutes in some small measure a belated tribute to their inspiration. Except where I have been given explicit permission by their families to use their real names I have, out of respect for their privacy, used pseudonyms. In some cases, where I have been unable to trace the families, I have altered some of the background details in an attempt to ensure that their anonymity is preserved. If any such families recognise themselves and the experiences we shared I hope they will forgive me for any offence or distress this may have caused. Rest assured it was not intended.

Wherever possible I have sought permission to quote from articles and letters. However, the absence of current addresses has meant that in some cases I have been unable to do so. If any of those people, whose letters meant, and still mean so much to me, care to get in touch I shall be glad to acknowledge them in any future editions of this work.

Stephen Turnbull first suggested in 1982 that I write a book. John Emery insisted that the bereavement care I was trying to offer be replicated throughout the country. Elisabeth Kübler-Ross urged me to disseminate my "five Ts of bereavement first aid" (even if tea in the U.S.A. becomes coffee or Coke). I still have the butterfly and the four-leaf clover she gave me as tokens of encouragement in my work.

Jill and Ronald Russell have been invaluable in providing a haven of peace in which to write. They have also been generous in their support and gentle in their comments on the draft chapters, as have Anne and Tim Penton, Anne and Tom Bragg, and Chris Deacon.

There are many colleagues, in any number of professions, without whose belief in what I have been trying to do I could never have kept going. In naming some I am in danger of causing offence by omitting others: Peter Page, Mary Holder, John Scott, John Gallagher, Ross Mitchell, Nick Stevenson, Sue Robinson, Howard Sherriff, Chris Constant, Mark Farrington, Martin Johns, Gilbert Park, Yvonne Sangster, Maurice James, Jim Rone, Chris Burton, Austin Gresham, Roy Calne, Duncan Walker, Tony and Hilary Scase.

It was only after the book was written and the title decided upon that I met Paul Sinclair who runs Motorcycle Funerals Limited[1]. I am grateful that he does not consider me to be a serious competitor to his specialised funeral service, and I am happy to recommend him to those who want a "Rolls Royce Sidecar" for their final journey.

---

1 *http://motorcyclefunerals.com*

Introduction

Death has been described as "the last taboo," which is bizarre in a society with a 100% mortality rate. This book endeavours to remove the false mystery and unnecessary fear surrounding this most unavoidable of phenomena. By drawing on the experience of people facing death, whether their own or that of those near to them, the author records their insights into what it is they want of us as neighbours, relatives, or carers.

The institutionalisation of death, he suggests, has contributed to the lack of experience in the population at large in dealing with the practical, emotional, and spiritual issues associated with it. These are all addressed in some detail. Questions such as "Why me? What have I done to deserve this? What will become of me when I die?" need to be acknowledged at a deeper level than by recourse to glib recitation of catechisms or other religious or philosophical statements.

A research project involving the author (without his knowledge) has demonstrated that elementary and timely bereavement care has resulted in dramatically better readjustment in the bereaved to their loss. Although this has been the subject of seminars for nurses, doctors, police officers, paramedics, and theological students for over 20 years this is the first time it has been presented for publication.

At a time when religious beliefs seem to be associated with international conflict this book seeks to demonstrate that there is an underlying spirituality which breaks through the barriers created by religion, culture, and language. It also reports on how inadequate is the religious thinking and practice of some self-styled Christians in the face of death. The response of many, whether they have any personal belief system or not, has been one of welcome towards the author's "un-churchy" approach.

Specific instances of out-of-body experience, poltergeist activity, and of the paranormal are recorded in detail for the first time. No conclusions are drawn, but the reader may well be challenged by the way the evidence is corroborated.

The book recognises and celebrates the element of humour that arises from even the most unlikely of circumstances. In the author's experience people seem to need permission to laugh as well as to weep, and this book encourages both.

Children's perceptions

School was hell. The nightmare lasted twelve years from the age of four, broken only by sleep and school holidays. One dour teacher insisted that it was the happiest time of your life. Fortunately he was mistaken.

My childhood home was in a small market town in Norfolk. Across the road was a builder's yard which was an Aladdin's Cave for an inquisitive small boy. My favourite part was the joinery shop. It had special smells. There were piles of wood shavings and sawdust smelling sharp and clean if the carpenter was working with pine, or sweet and rich if he was using oak. I was allowed to help stir the glue pot and it smelt very strange. Because I had been told not to get in the way I tried not to ask too many questions. For a long time my unspoken query was why all the houses that Berty Coleman was building had such funny-shaped wardrobes in them. My own room did not have a wardrobe — just a rail on which to hang my clothes behind a curtain. I had never seen wardrobes like these. There seemed to be a fundamental design fault in that the doors were not fitted with hinges, but instead had four big screws in them. I had never seen wardrobes with brass plates on the doors declaring whose clothes were inside. Like so many builders Berty Coleman was also the local undertaker, and I had been given my first carpentry lessons making coffins.

Soon after I was ordained my boss, the vicar, told me that I must spend a morning a week teaching in the local school. He could have had no idea the contortions my guts went through on hearing this. The smell of varnished floors, of damp coats, of chalk dust, and of institutional cooked vegetables—all these when compounded by the sound of peremptory voices calling children to order triggered memories in me that made me want to turn and run. Why did I not do so? Partly because I would have had to face the wrath of the vicar, but partly because I was desperate to give the thirty ten- and eleven-year-olds in front of me a positive experience of teaching and learning.

Things started badly. I had been told to instruct the children on "The Christian Year". They wasted no time in demolishing my teaching plan. "What's wrong with the ordinary year?" It was an eminently reasonable question to which the answer had to be "There's nothing wrong with it." Working on the principle that if you can't beat them, join them, I asked them what they wanted me to tell them about. To this day I cannot remember who broke the silence which followed. Somewhere there was a young voice saying "Heaven." Suddenly there was a chorus of voices all shouting "Yes! Tell us about Heaven." The class teacher, recognising my fear of taking his class, had kindly offered to sit at the back of the class to provide moral support. The look on his face was eloquent. He was as surprised as I was at the children's response, and his grin proclaimed his thought "Now you have dropped yourself in it, right up to your neck." In order to buy time I invited the children to write down their questions about Heaven. One of them produced an empty cornflakes box from the store. The pieces of paper bearing the questions were put into the box for safe keeping, and for the rest of term each Friday morning was spent delving into the cereal packet and trying to address the questions posed by the young theologians.

"Do people have wings in Heaven?"

"Do they eat food?"

"Do they talk?"

"Do they stay the same age?"

"Do murderers go to Heaven?"

"Is Heaven in colour?"

In 1969 not many households had colour television. I was left in no doubt that if Heaven was only in black and white God was going to have to return to the drawing board and redesign it in colour!

"Do we see people who have died in our minds or in real life?"

"How do we get to Heaven?"

"If you can't see God now how can you see him in Heaven, because you said Heaven is all around us?"

I decided that this question was best addressed by means of a practical exercise. We all put on our coats and went into the school playground. It was a foggy November morning. I gave a whistle to one child and told him to walk across the playground to the netball post on the other side. He disappeared into the fog. "Where is he?" I asked.

"He's bunked off home" was the reply. The class teacher told me later that he was for ever playing truant. More in hope than in confidence I called out "Blow your whistle." He did, and the children all shouted "He's there!" We all returned to the classroom, shed our coats and considered our experience. We had just demonstrated that eyesight is not the only sense we have to let us know of the presence of things unseen.

The children were fascinated at the way their parents reacted when told what we had been talking about in school. One boy told us that during the week his nan and grandad had been staying at his house and he had been telling them what we were talking about in school, "dying and Heaven and all that." His grandad had said you shouldn't talk about that kind of thing. He added, as if disagreeing with his grandfather, "But why not?"

"Yes — why not?" joined in everyone else.

"Dying isn't something to be frightened of" said the boy with the grandfather. "It's just the end of Part One." There was general laughter as a girl got up from her desk and paraded round the classroom distributing imaginary ice creams during the interval before the beginning of Part Two.

I wonder how many of these children, now old enough to have ten-year-olds of their own, still remember our Friday mornings with the cornflakes box. I remember them with gratitude for their directness and insight whenever I am conducting a funeral at the crematorium. For all the sadness of parting as the curtains close in front of the coffin I hear in my mind's ear "It's the end of Part One." And I hope that the person to whom we are saying "Goodbye" is enjoying Part Two, with or without ice cream.

Some years later, in another school and in a different town, I was invited by the personal tutor of a group of sixteen-year-olds to tackle some issues they had put together. After initial testing of the water with questions like "If God's your boss how do you get paid?" we got down to serious stuff. "What do you think of people who sell themselves?"

"You're asking my opinion on prostitution, are you?" Clearly they were, but they lacked the nerve to use the word. I responded quietly by explaining that I did not know very many prostitutes, but that those I did know, both male and female, were without exception lonely and sad people. This was clearly not the response the young people were expecting from me and they interrogated me further. Why were they sad and lonely? I suggested that it might be that any relationships they had were simply to meet their clients' needs — that people tended to use them, and abuse them, for the service they could provide rather than because they were intrinsically loveable and valuable people in their own right. The discussion moved nearer to home when one or two girls in the class had the courage to explain that this was rather the way they felt when under pressure from their boyfriends. After a while one of the young men, possibly feeling threatened by the discussion, changed the subject by asking if I prayed and whether prayer worked. Having checked that everyone else was content that we address this, I tried to assess their perception of prayer. Was it a shopping list you gave to God? Were you trying to twist his arm against his better judgement in order to get your own way? It was clear that here was another intimate subject about which they had never had the chance to reflect. In an effort to give them a concrete example to discuss I told them about a friend of mine. He had children much the same age as the members of the class. For some weeks he had been getting weaker and, over the last few days, had begun to lose the sight in one of his eyes. As we spoke he was in hospital undergoing brain surgery. Already he would have been unconscious and there was nothing I could do for his material needs. However my whole being longed for his survival from hazardous surgery, for the restoration of his sight and mobility, and for the courage and comfort of his wife and children. Most of all at that moment my prayer was for a surgeon and theatre team I had never met and who would not have a clue who I was.

At this point the school bell rang, indicating that it was time for lunch. The class was slow to leave the room. As they filed past me several of the young men and women made comments like "I hope he gets better," and "I'll pray for him and his family."

Weeks later, when he was recovering at home, his sight restored, he described to me how he had felt just before being anaesthetised. With his arms outstretched in front of him, the palms of his hands up, Derek said he felt as if he had been carried and lifted up by people's love.

A couple of years later I was working full time in hospital chaplaincy. I came across Tony soon after his motorcycle accident. One leg had been amputated and one arm hung limp and useless because the nerves controlling movement had been damaged in the crash. As I passed by his bed on my way to see another patient I noticed that Tony looked particularly depressed. The staff agreed that they, too, were concerned about his state of mind. Because I had another commitment I could not give Tony much time that morning, but I promised I would look in on him later in the day. Unknown to him, and indeed unknown to any of the staff on the ward, I was due to spend the day away from the hospital with a community of nuns in quiet prayer. That evening I carried out my promise to visit Tony again. Although still feeling low, he said he felt a bit brighter, as if there had been people willing him to get better. I smiled and explained that I had spent the day with others praying for him and Jenny, his wife. Our longing was that they find the strength and courage to face whatever was ahead of them.

He looked at me in disbelief.

"Well, I'll be damned," he said. "I never realized that prayer worked!"

The last news I had of them was that they had been seen at a disco. Tony was getting around well on his artificial leg, with his limp arm tucked round Jenny's waist.

Holy water

An Englishman, an Irishman, and a Scotsman were reading the British Medical Journal. Over coffee and mince pies we were considering a report of the case of a young man recovering from multiple injuries in hospital. Six weeks after admission to a major injuries unit the patient's condition had deteriorated suddenly and he was found to be suffering from an overwhelming infection of *Pseudomonus aeruginosa*. My colleagues in this informal seminar, both surgeons, told me that this sort of bug was usually found in dirty water and drains. For it to turn up in an intensive care unit was very worrying. The article reported that the authors, Ian Greaves and Ken Porter, had been unable to find a source of this infection until one of them noticed the patient's aunt sprinkling him liberally with holy water. She was immediately stopped and the remaining water was sent for microbiological investigation. This revealed that the same bug that had made the patient so ill was also present in the holy water. "Once the situation was explained the aunt immediately stopped sprinkling with holy water." It had been a fortunate coincidence that, in this case, the source of infection had been located. The authors of the article suspected that such transmission of life-threatening infection is more common than realised.

As we ate our way through mince pies and drank coffee made from freshly boiled water we considered the implications for our own hospital. Not only do we have several intensive care units containing critically ill patients, but we also have other areas where there are people whose ability to resist infection is low. I reported that I had noticed plastic bottles on bedside lockers which were alleged to contain holy water. We were not calling into question the holiness of the water or its possible purity when originally bottled. However we were uneasy about what bugs might grow in an unsealed container stored at room temperature for months on end. Following our meeting I wrote a memorandum to the chairman of our hospital's infection control committee.

"My attention has been drawn to the B.M.J. volume 305, 19-26 December, 1992. In it a case of pseudomonal infection is described, attributed to the use by a patient's relative of holy water.

At an *ad hock* (sic) meeting between Mr C.R.C., Mr H.M.S., and myself, representing notionally the Roman Catholic, Free Church, and Anglican traditions, we concluded that a revision of hospital protocol in the use of holy water might be indicated. It was suggested that infection might be avoided if a transport medium of at least 60% alcohol was used for the holy water. Gin or vodka were the media of choice, with single malt strongly contra indicated. This was because tainting the malt with holy water was considered sacrilegious to the whisky.

I would welcome your consideration of this suggestion, preferably at a meeting in which we could determine by experiment the best transport medium."

This memo was written on December 31. By January 5 the head of the local Public Health Laboratory Service had sent me his reply.

⧄DDENBROOKE'S

CLINICAL MICROBIOLOGY AND PUBLIC HEALTH LABORATORY
ADDENBROOKE'S HOSPITAL,
HILLS ROAD,
CAMBRIDGE. CB2 2QW

Rev. Ian Morris
Chaplain
Addenbrooke's Hospital.

4/1/93

Dear Reverend Morris,

Holy Water

Thank you very much for your memo about this - it enlivened an otherwise rather tedious and routine morning's work.

I concur with most of the deliberations of your *ad hock* committee. Particularly so with regard to the possible transport media, although I'd suggest the suitability of single malt whisky should be studied in depth and repeatedly before it was rejected.

Surely what we need is a Spiritual Sterilizing Working Party ? This (self-selecting) group can exhausively assess the 60% alcohol proposal, and other more prosaic suggestions such as blessing sterile water, sterilizing blessed water, and warning visitors not to spray pseudomonas soup around the hospital. Are blessings stable after autoclaving at 121°C for 10 minutes ? Do they pass 0.45μm filters ? Will you need to bless our laboratory autoclaves ?

I shall bring this forward at the next meeting of the Infection Control Committee (it will make a pleasant change from all the wrangling about Hepatitis B vaccination and MRSA outbreaks) - perhaps you could give me a ring sometime in the near future so we can make sure that practices in Addenbrooke's really are safe ? I carry bleep 362, and can usually be reached via hospital extension 8548.

Yours aseptically,

Dr M Farrington
Consultant Microbiologist and Infection
Control Doctor.

A couple of weeks later I received a letter from one of my colleagues at our original meeting.

"Dear Ian,

<u>Re Holy Water</u>

Thank you for the copy of your memo to Dr M.F. relating to the problems of 'Holy Water'. First of all I am delighted to see the ecumenism we have in this hospital where one minister can represent so many churches.

I do have one problem regarding the use of alcoholic transport media. I personally (as only I can 'personally' be) am a tea-totaller. I would point out that I do not drink tea but I do not drink alcohol either. Perhaps you could tell me how the use of Coca-Cola would affect Holy Water both religiously and bacteriologically as this would be my preferred medium. On a religious level perhaps you could also advise me whether the use of alcohol in Holy Water would contravene my tea-total principles.

Many thanks,
Yours sincerely,
C.R.C."

By the same post I received another letter from the head of the Public Health Laboratory Service.

"Could I briefly uncork the holy water bottle again? One of my colleagues has raised an interesting point. Sprinkling from a bottle or other container will not cause a problem, but he thinks a brush-like arrangement (could this be an 'aspergillum'?) is used to do the spraying. If so, this can be a source of bugs, and I'd prefer aspergillum-free sprinkling.

Could you come back to me on this? I enclose a first draft of something we might circulate.
Yours sincerely,
M.F."

The draft guidelines to high-dependency units in the hospital included the following.

"Sprinkling of Holy Water by relatives of hospital patients is not to be encouraged because of the likelihood of bacterial contamination in bottled waters. However, if relatives nevertheless wish to sprinkle Holy Water either

1) pharmacy-supplied sterile water that has been blessed can be used,

2) the Clinical Microbiology and Public Health Laboratory is willing to autoclave Holy Water and return it in small volume sterile containers. (Please contact the head MLSO).

Each container of Holy Water should be used only once within a single 24 hour period and then discarded."

My own research on the wards led me to the conclusion that "aspergilla" were not generally used as the method of application of holy water in hospital. They were reserved for use in church, and I was reminded of how, in my youth, I had insisted on wearing a raincoat in church even in dry weather. This was because when the parish priest went up and down the church wielding what looked like a dish mop I always got soaked. In hospital the holy water tended either to be drunk by the patient or applied topically (rubbed on the affected part) either by the patient or by relatives. A nursing colleague was witness to a potentially fatal incident when a relative tried to give a patient holy water to drink. The problem lay in the fact that the patient had suffered a stroke and had lost his swallowing reflex. As a result the holy water went down the wrong way and he choked. Swift clinical intervention saved his life.

Upon mature reflection I concluded that neither alcohol nor Coca-Cola were very wise as transport media, for the simple reason that, when sprinkled, rubbed, or otherwise applied to the patient, they left a sticky mess.

The whole subject had arisen in a light-hearted way as the three of us were trying to wind down before Christmas; I suspect that a more "earnest" approach to the Infection Control Committee might have received a less sympathetic response. In the event we achieved in four months a review of infection control policy and a hospital protocol on the use of holy water which respects people's religious scruples and yet which avoids the risk of infection described in the B.M.J.

Some months later I was witness to a heated discussion in one of the hospital's passenger lifts. A member of the Public Health Laboratory Service and someone working for the Medical Research Council travelled up and down the ten floors several times as other passengers listened bemused to their argument. Each was claiming that the autoclaves in their respective departments were more efficient at removing the bugs while retaining the efficacy of the holy water. I was called upon to set up a "double blind" experiment in order to determine whether autoclaving reduced the sanctity of the water. I declined, not least because I foresaw with dread the Contracts Department trying to establish quality targets and purchase orders for holy water.

The staff in our Medical Illustration and Photography department rounded the topic off nicely with the following cartoon.

"I'm alive"

Pat was 32. She and her husband Tony had two young children. She also had a particularly nasty form of lung cancer. Since there was no further clinical treatment appropriate she had been discharged home from hospital into the care of her family and G.P. One Saturday afternoon the staff nurse in charge of the ward on which Pat had stayed called me. "Pat has turned up demanding that we find her a faith healer. Can you help?"

I went to the ward to find Pat, sitting in the wheelchair which Tony had used to get her from the car park, looking white-faced, wide-eyed, and near panic. She reiterated her demand that I find her a faith healer. It is not that I lack any faith in faith healers, but rather that I did not know anyone appropriate to meet Pat's needs that Saturday afternoon. Instead I suggested that she, Tony, Staff Nurse, and I should set to in Sister's office with a large pot of tea and a box of tissues. Suspecting that much of her panic stemmed from Pat's feeling that the whole situation was outside her control I made a suggestion.

"Let us assume, just for the moment, that you don't have very much longer to live. What I would like you to do is to make a list of all the things that are important for you to say and do and achieve in the time you do have. We can then work through that list and decide which things need to be done while you still have the energy to do them, and what can wait until later."

Pat laughed at me, but I kept my pen poised above the piece of paper in front of me. Realising that I was not joking she said quietly "I want Tony to know how much I love him."

The two of them hugged and wept with each other. Staff Nurse, who was herself newly married, and I took advantage of the box of tissues. I made a great show of writing down Pat's first objective, and after the tears had subsided I looked up and said "I think I can put a tick against that one, can't I?"

They laughed and agreed, and the rest of the list tumbled out: some days together with the children at the seaside, a visit to aged grandparents, and to numerous friends. At the end of an hour the teapot and all of us were exhausted. The list was now in Pat's control. She stuffed it into the pocket of her anorak, and we walked out to their car. As she climbed into the front passenger seat she said "I don't need a faith healer now."

I grinned and asked Tony if he wanted me to go back to the ward to collect the wheelchair.

There was no magic in this incident. All I had tried to do was to help her see that, even if she did have a life-limiting condition she continued to be a person in her own right. She had not been written off. She helped me to understand that dying is something that happens to people who are alive. Their greatest fear is of being treated like they are dead before they have died. She had some living to do and with our encouragement she was going to do it. In the event she managed the holiday at the seaside. She visited the relatives and friends, and she died a couple of weeks later, knowing that her husband loved her.

It was not panic but indignation which overwhelmed Sylvia. She had been in hospital receiving radiotherapy. She understood that the treatment would not cure her, but that it might shrink the tumour enough to keep her free of symptoms for a few more months. In the event the side effects were too bad to endure. One morning a junior doctor discussed the treatment with Sylvia and they agreed that it was time to stop the radiotherapy and get her home to her family. While she was waiting on the ward for her husband to collect her the consultant began his ward round. Sylvia noticed him start with the patient at one end of her "Nightingale" ward, with fifteen beds down each side. He moved to the next bed, and then the next. As he finished discussing the woman in the bed to her left he passed by the end of her bed without even looking at her. It is said that Hell hath no fury like a woman scorned. Sylvia was livid. She was a diabetic and she had to use small lancet needles to stab her finger in order to produce a drop of blood so that she could check her blood sugar. She reached into her bedside locker for one of these lancets, removed it from its sterile envelope, and rammed it into the buttock of her consultant who was beside the bed of her neighbour on the right.

"Damn you," she exclaimed. "I'm alive! Treat me like I'm alive!" To his credit, when he could sit down the consultant did so on the edge of her bed and apologized for passing her by.

David knew that he would never leave hospital. He had motor neurone disease. His mind was as clear as ever, but his ability to speak and move was failing fast. Because talking was a struggle for him, not just in the physical effort, but in the frustration of making himself understood, I often used to sit beside him in what I called "companionable silence". One day it was evident that he wanted to say something and so I made it clear that I had all the time he needed. Syllable by syllable he put the words together. Because he had lost his swallowing reflex I had to use a suction tube every few minutes to remove his saliva. Finally I understood his question. It had taken him forty minutes to ask me "What is going to happen when I die?" I knew that he had been brought up within the Roman Catholic tradition and so I allowed for this in my answer. "Am I right in thinking that your question 'What is going to happen?' has several parts to it?" He blinked twice which meant "Yes."

"You could be asking me what is going to be the event which causes you to die. You could also be asking me about what will be going on around you. And you could be asking what is going to happen to you afterwards." To each of these he blinked twice. Trusting that I was pitching my answers at the correct level for a man I had come to know and respect over several months I set to.

"You know and I know that there is a possibility you may choke. We try to have someone near you at all times so that we can suck you out quickly. But if that fails we have a single dose of medicine ready to give you straight into the cannula in your hand in order to lift you out of any distress."

I think I detected surprise in his eyes that even the hospital chaplain on the ward was aware of the contingencies David might require. I hope he found it reassuring. Secondly," I said, "I hope there'll be someone beside you, whether it's your wife or one of us, ready to keep you company for as long as you need us. And thirdly, I have a hunch that you may be somewhere over by the door, looking back down at your body in the bed, and wondering what the hell we are all doing crying." There was no doubt that he was smiling with his eyes.

In the event he did not choke. He died very peacefully in his sleep. So I was wrong as to the first part of my answer to David's question. There was someone sitting quietly beside him as his breathing became imperceptible and then stopped. At least I got that bit right.

As to whether the third part of my answer was correct, I shall have to wait until I can ask him in Heaven!

Having agreed to accompany H. to theatre where she was to have a laryngectomy I was the last person to hear her speak. Once she had recovered from the anaesthetic and surgery she would hold conversations by means of a notepad. One evening when I was sitting beside her bed it was clear to me that she was angry. With impatience she wrote on the pad

> I may be dumb.

> I may be dying.

> **BUT I AM NOT DAFT!**

The last line was written with such force that the imprint of the words was visible for ten pages. With support H. was coming to terms with her life-limiting condition. Until the speech therapist had been able to teach her a new way of voicing her words she used a notepad. But what she could not and would not tolerate was being treated as if she was an imbecile—"doolally" to use her term. Some visitors had apparently sat round her bed presuming that if she could not reply to their questions then she must be stupid. It had been a classic case of "Does he take sugar?" which, for H. had, in addition to the insult, the fear that she might be treated with such lack of consideration and dignity as she became weaker and died.

Pat, Sylvia, David, and H. had each needed reassurance that their dignity and autonomy—their being themselves—would be respected for as long as they had any living to do. Each of them had been given some warning that they might not have long to live, even if, like most of us, they found it necessary to deny this at least some of the time. For one man, whose name I never discovered, it all happened very suddenly.

It had taken the Fire Service an hour and a half to extricate him from his car following a road traffic accident. He lay on a trolley in the Accident and Emergency Department while the Trauma Team was working out what was wrong with him and in what order they should try to patch him up. He declined to speak, yet he hung on tight to anyone near him. This could have compromised the efforts of the skilled staff when carrying out their tasks in preparing him for the operating theatre. My hand was acceptable and unskilled, and so I sat on a stool beside him.

After a while he said "All these people in white coats — they're no use to me. They're just baffled technicians."

I gulped and thought "We've assembled our whole Trauma Team for you." But I did not say that. Instead I invited him to enlarge on what he had told me.

"They've got written all over them 'I am a failure'."

"Oops!" I thought. "This guy's hallucinating. His blood oxygen must be dropping." Instead of saying anything I nodded as if to encourage him. He went on "I don't feel as if I have much more humanity left, but I need to know that what little I have is legal tender."

"It sounds as if you feel that there has been a run on the humanity market, and you need someone to invest in your humanity."

"Yes," he replied. "More than anything else I need someone who looks as if he understands."

His grip loosened on my hand, his eyes closed, and the cardiac monitor trace went flat. His spleen had ruptured and he died then and there. We were baffled technicians. From a clinical point of view we had written all over our faces "We have failed him".

The question I faced as I left the department was "Have I been what you needed most—someone who looks as if he understands?"

Control

People imagine that having a religious belief somehow makes it easier to face dying and death. I have never found any research that supports this notion. Indeed, there is a lot of evidence to suggest that those who have spent a lifetime being "very religious" feel badly let down as they approach the end of their lives.

The staff on a coronary care unit had noticed that one of the patients in the unit seemed to be frantically busy looking through her bible. A nurse, concerned at the woman's agitation, asked her if she would appreciate a visit from the chaplain. This made her even more frantic and she declined the offer. The staff then put out a bleep call for me, inviting me to join them for coffee. "What's the hidden agenda?" I asked.

"Bring some Jaffacakes and we'll tell you" was the cryptic reply.

I walked through the coronary care unit to the staff office in which were the heart monitoring equipment, coffee making facilities, a refrigerator, and all the clutter associated with busy people working on a ward of acutely ill people. The refrigerator door had inscribed on it a number of graffiti, including one in my daughter's hand: "Life is a sexually transmitted disease which is invariably fatal because it comes in biodegradable packages." Over coffee and biscuits I was briefed about the woman with the bible. She had suffered quite a severe heart attack and it was desirable that she be exposed to as little stress and anxiety as possible at this stage. Because she had been offered contact with the chaplain and had turned it down I was now stuck. I could not approach her without going against her expressed wishes. This incident demonstrated to the staff the consequence of asking an apparently innocent question

"Would you like a visit from the chaplain?" If the answer, based on ignorance of the way the chaplain works, is "No", then the door is shut and only the patient can open it again. Reaching across the desk for another Jaffacake a staff nurse accidentally knocked over my coffee mug. The contents spilled on to my thigh and, although not scalding me, left me decidedly incontinent of coffee. There was much laughter as I crossed the ward and headed for the sluice where I hoped to dry off and recover some semblance of dignity. The woman with the heart attack and bible noticed the hilarity and I acknowledged her with a smile as I passed the end of her bed. After drying my trousers I left the ward and had just reached the lift when my bleep went off. The woman in question had decided that she would like to see me after all. I pulled up a chair and sat down beside her bed. It appears that the laughter and my smile had modified her expectation of the chaplain enough for her to risk contact.

She had been brought up within a very strict Christian tradition. Apparently the bible provided all the answers to life's questions—until now. She was frightened of dying and ashamed of having to admit it. She assumed that her life of religious observance and reading the bible would equip her for every eventuality. She concluded that her fear must be the consequence of her sinful lack of faith, and she admitted that she had been afraid I would condemn her for her failure to put her trust in God. Gently I asked her if she recalled the episode after The Last Supper, when Jesus took his close friends into the Garden of Gethsemane. He knew he did not have long to live and he begged them to hang in with him. I had jogged her memory enough for her to recall the record of Jesus on his knees with great beads of sweat rolling down his face.

"Do you think perhaps he knows how you've been feeling?" I asked her. "Can you take any comfort from the idea that if he was frightened, then you are allowed to be as well? It's no sign of lack of faith—just a matter of being realistic and human."

She had closed her bible. Her shoulders were less hunched up, and her voice sounded less strangled. "I'd never thought of it like that," she said. "So when Jesus cried from the cross 'My God! Why have you forsaken me?' he really meant it."

I agreed that, at the time, he probably had felt forsaken. Was that how she felt? She turned the tables on me by replying that she *had* felt forsaken, but that she didn't any longer. The spilt coffee had been a blessing in disguise.

On another ward lay another patient. She, too, had been brought up to think that illness and disability were visitations from a vengeful god. Gladys was blind. That in itself was interpreted as dramatic evidence that she must have been very wicked at some stage in her life. Now cancer was bringing her life to an end. Two such punishments in life, as she had been taught to believe, meant that the only place for her after death was Hell. Within ten minutes of first meeting her I concluded that she was a lovely lady burdened not only by an acute phase of depression but also by decades of indoctrination into a particular mindset in which fear of Hell was given greater precedence than love of Heaven. I suspected that Gladys was more frightened of what would happen to her after death than of death itself. Yet she spoke with such affection of neighbours and of the staff caring for her that I concluded that she was a loving and generous person.

"Gladys," I said. "I have only known you for a few minutes, but already I have the impression that you would be entirely out of place in Hell. You're such a lovely and loving person that you would make it hell for everyone else who was there simply because you would show them all up and make them feel ashamed of their selfishness."

She looked shocked. I had taken a risk in demolishing her religious preconceptions built up over a lifetime. There are those who might accuse me of arrogance in trying to replace her religious structure with another one of my own. In my defence I can only appeal to the outcome. The staff who had asked me to visit her because she had been so withdrawn and depressed now commented on how much brighter she seemed. She came to recognise my footfall as I entered her room. "Is that you, Ian love?" she would say, feeling for my hand as I sat down beside her.

A couple of days before she died, although, of course, at the time I could not have known it would be so soon, I felt that her perception of herself and of her destiny was sufficiently positive for me to be able to invite her to take an active role rather than being permanently passive—a "patient".

"Gladys. May I ask you a favour?"

"Go on, love. What is it?"

"I'm sure you'll be ever so happy and busy in Heaven. But I wonder whether, if you've got time and if you feel so inclined, you could put in a good word for me. I'd be quite content with a little stool by the gate where I could use my oil can to stop the hinges from squeaking."

"No," she replied, taking my hand. "I'll ask for a place right next to me."

There are those for whom being "very religious" means that certain rituals have to be performed exactly as they always have been, whatever the circumstances. A woman came into my office to tell me about her husband who had been admitted to hospital. He had suffered a severe stroke and, as a result, had lost his speech and swallowing reflex. I was instructed that he must receive Holy Communion every morning before breakfast from an Anglican priest, who, by her definition, had to be male.

As I listened I was trying to allow for her anxiety for her husband, and her desire to cling to any semblance of normal routine in their life. However there was a niggle at the back of my mind. Was I in the presence of a control freak— someone for whom ritual practices were not so much an expression of devotion to God but instead a means of trying to control him and the rest of nature? I have to admit to a passing thought that she might have wanted her husband to choke when receiving the bread and wine, and thus speed him on his way to Heaven. As I looked at her I let my eyes drift out of focus, as if gazing beyond her. My suspicion was confirmed when she demanded "What are you thinking?"

"Since you ask," I replied "I was wondering how the hell you're going to manage if, when you get there, you find that Heaven isn't exactly to your taste."

Predictably she went into orbit and stormed out of my office.

Later that day I developed cold feet and made a telephone call to her parish priest outlining the conversation. I admitted that I might have been too blunt with her.

"Oh Ian!" he replied. "I've been longing to say that to her for years!"

Person specification

An eleven-year-old was due to have surgery. His family were understandably anxious but they were not helping him by the way they all sat around his bed as if at his wake. It was the evening before the date scheduled for his operation. As I wandered past his bed he called out to me "Uncle Ian. I don't want to go to the slaughterhouse on my own!"

I found a space to sit on his bed and explained that he would not go to the operating theatre on his own. His favourite nurse would go with him.

"I'd feel better if you came too."

"O.K." I replied. "I'll see you in the morning."

"Will you stay?"

"You'll be fast asleep. You won't notice if I'm there."

"I'd still feel better if you stay."

"Right. I'll stay with you."

The next morning the theatre porter and I turned up to collect him. He hung on to my hand very tight until he was asleep. It was a privilege to observe, with running commentary, as skilled hands rectified what nature had got wrong.

During one of the more routine parts of the procedure the surgeon asked me what I considered were the essential characteristics required of a hospital chaplain. I could have done with notice of the question in order to do it justice. However I gave it my best shot and listed three, although not in any order of importance. The first essential was very considerable physical and emotional stamina. The second was the kind of religious faith which does not have to be worn on the sleeve. And the third was a sense of humour, however outrageous. It was during the discussion in which most of the theatre team took part that I learned the nickname which had been given to another hospital chaplain of their acquaintance—"Creeping Jesus". I am surprised the laughter which followed did not wake our unconscious patient.

The final sutures were in place and the anaesthetist adjusted the controls beside him. The boy's eyelids flickered and as he looked up from the operating table he said in a bleary voice "Uncle Ian, have they done it?" He did not wait for my answer before drifting back off to sleep. He made a good recovery from the surgery and was discharged home in ten days. When he returned some weeks later for an outpatient check-up he ran up to me and exclaimed "Uncle Ian, I can swim 25 metres." Not bad for someone who, before surgery, would have had a struggle to walk 25 paces.

The emotional stamina was required when a seven-year-old died on the self-same operating table. Not only was there the personal pain at seeing the still and lifeless form of a child. There was the pain behind the masks of everyone in the operating theatre who had been engaged in the common cause of trying to save his life. The surgeon, looking exhausted, said simply "What the bloody hell's your boss doing, taking Thursday half day?" His next task was to tell the lad's parents that he had died.

The challenge to my emotional and spiritual stamina did not end with those parents collecting up his "Get well" cards and other belongings and leaving the hospital. They had asked me to conduct his funeral. This meant that I was going to have to stand in front of his coffin, containing my own sadness, in order to support his family and friends, and to speak of my own perception of a Love big enough to keep him whole and safe in Heaven. The burial took place in a mining village during the 1984 miners' strike. The whole community had been brought to the very brink of despair by the apparent no-win situation they were in. And now this. Not only were the government and the leadership of their union perceived as being set on breaking their spirit. Now God had kicked them in the teeth as well, and I was supposed to be on his side. Having laid the lad to rest in his grave I walked, exhausted, back to the church. Suddenly my bleep went off with a voice message requesting that I ring the hospital. I looked up to meet the eyes of a fellow mourner, one of the miners. He had heard my bleep and he said "Eeh lad! We'll 'ave thee dahn our club. Ah didn't see tha lips move."

His prophecy was fulfilled some weeks later when I received an invitation to the miners' welfare club in the village. On behalf of the hospital I was to receive a gift of money raised in memory of the miner's son whose funeral I had taken. The culture and customs of Yorkshire miners' welfare clubs had formed no part of my training. It was therefore a completely new experience to find myself on the stage in front of 400 or so miners and their families. The compère introduced me, the Hammond organ played me in, and I was on my own. Except that I was not alone. Some weeks earlier we had shared each other's grief. This evening I was among the same people and we had something positive to share. The ripple of conversation continued as I began. "It's clear to me that you haven't heard the news flash I've just picked up on the car radio on my way down here. The Prime Minister has died..." The silence was absolute — "... and has arrived at the gates of Heaven demanding entry." There was a murmur of laughter as the audience realized that I had caught them up in my act.

St Peter seemed unable to find her name in his book and Mrs Thatcher drummed her fingers impatiently on the gatepost.

After all, Norman St John Stevas always referred to her as "The Blessed Margaret", and so there *had* to be a place for her in Heaven. When it became clear that St Peter was having no success in finding her name she said in her usual stentorian voice "But there is no alternative". Now St Peter, who over the centuries had become very gentle, was narked at this. He slammed the book shut and said "Oh yes there is. On your bike. And if yours doesn't work take Norman's!" (It is alleged that Norman Tebbit advised those unable to find jobs to get on their bikes and take work wherever they could.)

Desperate to have an audience somewhere she got on the bike and bounced down the steps towards Hell, cussing and swearing as she went. When she was halfway down Lucifer heard the row and language which even he had never come across. He took out his binoculars and he could not believe his eyes. All her lifetime people had been wishing her in Hell and here she was! He welcomed her with open arms and set her to work.

However, three days later he was desperate. Now it takes something to drive the Devil to despair. He picked up the 'phone. "Peter," he said. "It's Lucifer here. Do you remember me? You know that dreadful woman you sent me. You'll have to take her back. I can't stand her. She's shut down three furnaces already!"

The hall erupted. Beer mugs and caps were thrown in the air. The howls of laughter drowned the noise of the Hammond organ, and the compère gave up trying to call for order. So far as I was concerned it was more important that these people be reminded, by their sense of humour, of their own value as people, than whether or not one or two politicians suffer from a bit of light-hearted lampoonery.

It was especially good to be hugged by the seven-year-old's parents, who had not laughed for weeks.

Eleventh commandment

It used to be widely held that there was an eleventh commandment, written especially for nurses. Moses, it appears, must have run out of stone after allegedly carving ten. The eleventh was "Thou shalt not get involved with thy patient." No one ever told thee what "getting involved with thy patient" meant, but thou wast not allowed to do it, and furthermore, if thou didst then thou wast a bad nurse. There was no commandment forbidding thee from feeling angry when discovering as thou started out for work on an early shift that some prat hadst nicked all four wheels off thy car. Nor wast there anything amiss in feeling aggrieved upon receipt of a snotty letter from thy bank manager foreclosing upon thine overdraft. But to be upset because a patient you have come to know and care about has died, *das ist verboten*.

I have a theory that this commandment developed in the middle of the twentieth century as a mechanism for dealing with the cost of caring. Student nurses looked to senior staff nurses and sisters as role models, wondering how they managed to keep going in the face of human anguish. Perhaps they imagined that the senior staff had somehow switched off their ability to feel emotional pain at the plight of those for whom they cared. Thus, they concluded that if they too were to become true professionals they would have to do the same. What I suspect they failed to realize was that if they succeeded in isolating themselves from pain they would inevitably cease to be able to appreciate and delight in joy. As a consequence there grew up a generation of nurses who, because no one challenged their presupposition, practised and taught that, in order to be a good nurse, you had to avoid getting touched by the suffering you saw. This, I suggest, resulted in what might be called emotional leprosy. People with leprosy lose sensation in their fingers and toes. They therefore cease to recognise when they have cut, crushed, or burned their fingers because the nerves no longer send messages of pain to the brain so that the muscles can respond by withdrawing the hand from danger. In time the fingers and toes suffer so much damage that they become stunted. People who persistently deny the emotional consequences of their work are in danger, like lepers, of ceasing to recognise the damage being done to them. Only when it is too late do they find that they have become hollow, cynical practitioners, untouched by either the sadness or the joy of anyone around them. Some are left with enough insight to despise themselves for having lost the flame of inspiration which led them into nursing in the first place—the passion to care for the sick, the vulnerable, and the dying. Fortunately for them and for those of us who may become patients most of that generation of nurses have retired. New cohorts of nurses find reference to the eleventh commandment at the least quaint, and at the worst contrary to good nursing practice. If I have diabetes I need to know that the nurses caring for me while I am unconscious after surgery will make sure that my blood sugar levels are checked and that I receive appropriate doses of insulin. Such technical competence is not an alternative to being concerned for my emotional welfare and that of my family. They are two essential components of what makes a good nurse. What I do *not* need while I am a patient is to be treated by people who, because they have failed to recognise that the letter from the bank manager has screwed them up, either take out their frustration on me or make errors of clinical judgement which endanger my health. Most of the time experienced staff in health care, as in other statutory and voluntary agencies, succeed in keeping a healthy balance between their objective professional skills and their ability to be humane—to care. It requires courage and good self-awareness to recognise when the balance is under strain. The police "agony message" is a good example.

I might have been helping a police traffic officer and a mortuary technician to clean up and make presentable the body of a young man, reeking of alcohol, and to try to determine his identity from any documents in his pockets. The police officer sets off for the address of the dead man, perhaps with no clue as to whom he will find. On arrival he finds the street settled down for the night, and so the option of checking with a neighbour is not open to him. Instead he has to bang on the door until he wakes someone within. It is a child, who starts crying. Then lights are turned on. A young female voice calls out "Who is it?"

"It's the police. May I come in?"

"What is it? What do you want?"

I do not know any police officer who in response to that question would shout through the letterbox "Did Darren live here, because if he did he doesn't any longer."

However well he tries to prepare himself, to rehearse the words, when the time comes and he sees a worried and frightened young woman with small children clinging to her legs crying "Where's Daddy?"—then it requires a supreme effort of self-control to ask the right questions in a way which assures the family of care and support but which does not duck the issue. At the time he achieves it. If she wants to go to the hospital to be with her husband then he will take her.

"What about the children?" she asks.

He has learnt that children often handle the fact of death with much less difficulty than do adults. What frightens children is deception, and being kept in the dark. He knows that there will be someone (me) waiting for them and prepared to look after the children while their mother has time on her own with their father if they get bored. He offers to help get the children dressed and, while doing so tries to find out from their mother if she has any friends, relatives, or neighbours she would like informed so that they can be ready for her when she returns from seeing her husband. As they set off he calls up Control, requesting that the mortuary be informed of their estimated time of arrival.

Meanwhile we have done our best to tidy up the abrasions on Darren's face and hands. The multiple fractures to his legs and pelvis are covered over. I try to enlist the help of a trained paediatric nurse experienced in caring for upset children. And we wait. Like the police officer, the mortuary technician and I often see intense grief and it hurts every time.

The police car arrives at the hospital. The occupants struggle to get out. Police cars often have locks on the rear doors and so there is a moment of panic before we open them from the outside. Sensing their mother's anxiety the children are subdued. We explain that we are taking them to a sitting room next to the chapel of rest. Aware that his wife may never have seen anyone who has died, other than possibly in American police TV films, I explain that Darren is next door lying as if on a bed. He is very still and beginning to get cool. She is welcome to sit with him, hold his hand, hug him, talk to him, and come and go as she wishes. She may find that her eyes play tricks on her, such that she thinks she can still see him breathing. The police officer has by now checked that Darren is ready to receive his family. The young woman walks stiffly through the doorway. Is she going to run to him, scream, run back out of the room, or faint?

"Why is Mummy crying?"

"Because she's sad."

"Why is she sad?"

"Because Daddy has died."

"Why has Daddy died?"

"Because he was in a car crash and his body was so badly damaged that we couldn't mend it, and he has died and we are sad."

The police officer tries to respond to these children as he would to his own. But if it were he who lay on that mortuary trolley who would there be to care for his wife and children?

A neighbour has arrived at the hospital. I collect her from Reception and take her to the sitting room next to the chapel of rest. The children recognise her and all the explanations we have given them tumble out. I am always moved by the matter of fact way children speak about death. There is nothing of the unctuous Uriah Heep in them. There are questions to be asked and information to be given about the involvement of the coroner. There is a form which requires signatures confirming Darren's identity, but the police officer knows that such formalities cannot be rushed.

Once she recognises that Darren is not going to wake up and that he really is not breathing his wife gives me a haunted look of exhaustion across his body and says "What happens now?"

I explain that the police officer will take her through the next steps. We return to the sitting room and he invites her to sign a form he has prepared, confirming that it is indeed Darren in the chapel of rest. He knows that some people become very angry at being required to carry out such a bureaucratic formality, but he has learnt that a gentle response helps defuse anger. "If you wake up suddenly one night and think 'It was all a dream. Darren will come home,' remember that you and I sat here tonight and you identified him to me. It isn't a dream, even though we all wish it was." He promises to keep in touch with her and to keep her informed of the progress of the coroner's investigation. We give her a telephone number to call if, while Darren's body is in the hospital, she wants to come and be with him. Then her neighbour gathers her children together and we see them to their car.

Meanwhile, back in the mortuary office, mugs of tea await the police officer and me. He was about to end a shift when he was detailed to attend this "Fatal" and it is now four hours later. He has obtained all the information available at this stage. He has acted professionally and has tried to use all his insights into human grief reactions in order to be supportive and humane. And it has cost him dear. Sitting in private among friends he can admit how much it hurt to see those little children; how similar in age they are to his own; how lost and vulnerable their young mother seemed. There is a moment of anger at the selfishness of people who drink and drive, followed by the reflection that, from a comment she made, Darren's wife had been expecting something like this to happen.

Fifteen minutes "unwinding" helps each of us to keep a balanced view of reality, to acknowledge the emotional cost, and to encourage each other in our individual professional skills which, when we work as a team, make difficult jobs easier. Perhaps student nurses in the 1950s never saw their senior colleagues using such practical mechanisms for acknowledging and then "letting go" the pain associated with caring well. After all, Sister's office was hallowed ground.

I can still clearly recall the sunny Saturday afternoon in 1969 when I had been called in to the local hospital to escort some teenagers to the chapel of rest. A friend of theirs had died when her boyfriend wrapped their car round a lamp post while driving high on marijuana. The sight of so much grief in such youngsters had left me with red eyes. I had been careful not to make a display of my tearfulness. That might have deflected some of them from addressing their own needs to having to address mine, and that would indeed have been unprofessional. When I had seen them off and locked up the mortuary I returned the keys to the switchboard receptionist. In an acid voice she said how unprofessional she thought it was for a priest of the church of God to be seen weeping. I looked at her and said as coolly as I could "I seem to recall that the shortest verse in the bible is just two words 'Jesus wept'. And if it's good enough for him, then it's good enough for me!"

I admit that, in my view, the one part of my behaviour during this episode that was unprofessional was that, with some irritation, I slammed the keys down on the reception desk and stormed out without signing them back in.

No one, in my experience, chooses to be overwhelmed. By definition the shock sneaks up and catches you in an ambush.

It was lunch time on Saturday. I was stationary on my motorcycle in a line of traffic waiting for a Right filter at traffic lights. There was an incredible bang and a pain in my back. I recall that everything did not "go black" as many people describe in such incidents. It did, however, seem to go very dark brown. I remember thinking "In a moment I'm going to feel and hear a crunch as a wheel crushes my crash helmet and head."

I came round lying in the road with what turned out to be the van which had rammed me from behind now ahead of me. A witness described me as a rag doll in crash helmet and leathers dropping eight feet down on to the road with a "dead cat bounce". I remember a local doctor checking whether my neck was broken. Then someone in uniform came into my field of vision. "I'm a nurse," she said. "Can I help?"

"Hello Karen," I said weakly.

She screamed.

It was no fault in her that she was suddenly disabled by the shock of recognising the victim. In the event she was able to help the ambulance paramedics scoop me on to the stretcher. On arrival in the accident and emergency department of my own hospital I was given kind and competent attention. It had been suspected that there were fractures to my neck, elbow, pelvis, and leg. In the event I was able to walk, or rather hobble, out of the department a couple of hours later. I rang the motorcycle breakers whom the police had called to collect the wreck of my bike so as to give details of my insurers. I got through and explained that I was the owner of the motorcycle they had collected earlier. There was total silence at the other end of the telephone.

"Are you there?" I asked.

"Yes," came the shaken reply. "But are you there?"

"Of course I am. What's the problem?"

"I thought you were dead!"

The point was that no one should have survived a crash like that.

In the course of two hours there were two competent people ambushed by shock. They were not behaving unprofessionally. Rather, I submit that they behaved far more appropriately by being honest that they were temporarily overwhelmed than by trying to pretend that they were unaffected. In the event both recovered their equilibrium and were able to do their jobs.

I am glad that we no longer teach or even remember the eleventh commandment.

Communication

In a seminar with senior nurses I asked what they valued most in chaplains on their wards. It did not take long for them to agree that it was in the area of human mortality that they most appreciated help. By this they meant not only the occasions of death on a ward, but also when there was news of a diagnosis with life-limiting implications. There is a risk that, if such requests from nursing staff were the only occasions chaplains were seen on the wards, we could justifiably be perceived as harbingers of death or vultures "in for the kill". A patient on a surgical ward had asked to speak to a chaplain. The ward staff put out a bleep call and I responded. To reach the patient in question I had to pass the beds of two other men. As I went past the first he shouted at me "You're the last person I want to see."

I stopped and acknowledged his frightened stare. Once I had collected myself after this verbal onslaught I replied gently but firmly "I will make sure that gets recorded in your notes, and when the time comes I'll do my very best to be here!"

He looked at me in total incomprehension. Then the man who had asked to see me, whom I had not yet met, began to chuckle. He was followed by the patient in the middle bed of the three who began to laugh. Finally the first man saw the joke behind my deliberate misunderstanding of his tirade, and he smiled sheepishly. The man I had been called to see was not dying. He simply wanted me to let his local vicar know that he had been admitted to hospital.

There was, however, an occasion when one of the ward sisters who had attended the seminar was at the end of her own resources which were considerable. She had a patient who was very near the end of her life, and now hardly conscious. Her husband wanted to share her last hour or so quietly beside her bed. However, their entire family with partners were also determined to be there as well. Sister had tried reason: "There isn't room for twelve of you in there." She had tried authority: "I must insist that you stop disturbing my patient by arguing so noisily around her bed." I would not want to cross swords with her, and so, when she bleeped me, outlined the problem and asked me to sort it out, I resisted the temptation to decline on the grounds that "if you can't get them out what chance do I stand?"

With trepidation I squeezed in through the door of the single room. All around the bed were sons, daughters, sons-in-law, daughters-in-law, and sitting in an armchair beside her was the woman's distraught husband silently stroking her head. Lying across the bed, crushing her mother's knees, was a 35-year-old daughter who sobbed "Oh Mum! You can't do this to your little Carrie on her birthday."

My briefing from the ward sister had convinced me that words and reasoning would be of no avail, and so without saying a word I squeezed past the foot of the bed and found a space near the head, on the opposite side from the husband. Like that I could see both him and her at once. I knelt down and held the patient's hand, and said nothing. For ten minutes Carrie continued to cry and reproach her mother for wrecking her birthday, not only today, but in each successive year, by dying on it. Then I suspect she realized that this tactic was not commanding my attention. Instead I continued to kneel silently beside her mother. Carrie then slipped from across her mother and knelt quietly beside the bed, near to her father's feet. Ten minutes later everyone had become silent, some standing against the wall, others kneeling around the bed. The silence was such that I could hear the very slight scraping noise of the louvre in the glass panel in the door being turned and, as I glanced across at the door I saw the astonished look on the face of the ward sister on the other side of it. After a further 20 minutes I had lost all sensation in my legs and feet. The patient's breathing was becoming shallower, and Carrie cried out "How much longer is this agony going to last?"

For the first time since entering the room 40 minutes earlier I spoke.

"The only agony Mother is suffering is at hearing your distress. Just give her ten more minutes of your loving."

Silence returned and—as it happened—exactly ten minutes later Carrie's mother died. I hauled myself up the bed head, having temporarily lost the use of my legs, leant over the pillow and kissed the husband's hand as it lay caressing his wife's forehead, and left the room. Perhaps it was wishful thinking on my part but the muffled sound of the family's tears sounded more genuine, less theatrical, than before. Sister was beside herself with curiosity as to how I had achieved what she had failed to do. My hunch had been that there were some fairly dysfunctional and manipulative members of the family who had no previous experience of bereavement. I presumed that for any of them to leave the room would constitute loss of face and the fear of it implying that they "didn't love Mother". Instead I offered them a model of silent loving which addressed the husband's need. They could adopt or reject that model. In the event they chose to adopt it and, judging by some of their comments as the family left the hospital, they were glad to have been offered it.

On an adjacent ward was a man in his fifties who was undergoing radiotherapy treatment. The staff had shown me a letter from his G.P. in which the patient's wife was quoted as insisting that her husband must not be told he was dying. What began as an informal discussion at the nurses' station about the ethical implications of having the terms of care for one's patient circumscribed by relatives developed into a consideration of whether I had a role with this couple. The next day I "happened by" the ward day room and in the course of a relaxed and easy conversation with the patient, discovered how concerned he was about his wife's ability to handle his illness. Again as if by chance, I turned up on the ward that evening to see him lying in bed being fed jelly by his wife. He raised his eyebrows between spoonfuls as if to say "See what I'm having to put up with?" She looked daggers at me and shook her head so violently that the jelly fell off the spoon on to the bedclothes. I tried a weak smile of greeting and left the room, returning to the nurses' station. The wife followed, spoon in hand.

"My husband's not to be told he's dying."

"I beg your pardon," I replied, feigning ignorance.

"I've left strict instructions that he's not to be told he's dying."

"I have no intention of telling him any such thing. Is he dying?"

All she could do was rehearse the same sentence which was getting us nowhere. I concluded by saying that he was no fool, and that he was well aware of the reason for radiotherapy, and it was not measles. I contrived an excuse to terminate this non-conversation and made my way to the doctor's office where I left a note for the consultant who I knew would be conducting a ward round the next morning.

At visiting time the next evening my bleep went off. The ward sister warned me that the patient's wife wanted my guts for garters because I had (apparently) told her husband that he was dying. Rather than have another non-conversation at the nurses' station within earshot of the patient I asked Sister if I could use the doctor's office for an interview with the wife. I arrived at the office and Sister brought in the irate wife and her friend. She launched into a tirade, the essence of which was that she was going to report me to the Archbishop of Canterbury, the Prime Minister, and the Pope for telling her husband that he was dying. While she stopped to take breath I explained that I had not been either on the ward, or indeed in the hospital that day until now, since I had been teaching in another hospital twenty-five miles away. It therefore could not have been anything to do with me.

"What actually happened," I explained, "was that Dr M. saw your husband at 9.20 this morning and asked him what he thought was happening. He replied that he knew he was dying and had known for six weeks. So it was not I or Dr M. who told your husband. He told us!"

She burst into tears and, right on time, Sister entered the office with a tray of tea.

The result of this interview was that lines of communication between the couple were restored. The patient explained to me that he usually planned events and holidays on behalf of both of them. He was distressed that the one thing he could not save his wife from having to plan unaided was his funeral. I suggested that this might not necessarily be so. Had he, I enquired, considered whether she might have a preference for his burial or cremation. What style of funeral director would he prefer to know was looking after her when he would not be there to support her—a formal and reserved type, or a personal and friendly type? We decided on a funeral director, and at the patient's invitation I rang him and outlined the scenario. He turned up at visiting time, as agreed, and without top hat, tails, or silver topped cane. He, the patient and his wife worked out the details of the funeral. The next day the patient explained to me that it was not only an enormous relief to know that there was someone so thoughtful to take care of his wife, but that there was something almost mischievous about writing a cheque for his own funeral expenses! In the event he was able to go home. The funeral director told me later that he had taken the couple out for a meal together some three weeks before the patient died.

I never did hear from the Archbishop, the Prime Minister, or the Pope.

Poltergeist activity

A 27-year-old had been taken home from work at lunchtime because he was feeling unwell. His wife returned home to find him lying unconscious on the floor beside their bed. She called an ambulance, and the paramedic crew, having attempted to resuscitate him, took them both to the Accident and Emergency Department. As it was becoming clear that her husband was not going to survive a staff nurse asked the young woman if there was anyone we could get to keep her company — friends, neighbours, relatives.

She replied "Ian lives a couple of doors from me and he works here."

"We've already sent for him" replied the nurse. The consultant in charge of the resuscitation attempt heard this conversation and, as I arrived in the department a minute or so later, he stopped me, gently put his hand on my shoulder and said "Ian, we think you may find this rather tough. You know this young man, so we've sent for back-up for you."

It is that kind of thoughtful camaraderie which gives one the strength and courage to carry on in such stressful circumstances. In the event I was welcomed by Anne as she told me what had happened to Steve. For weeks he had been upset that his epilepsy did not appear to be responding to treatment, and he was worried that this might affect his career. He had waved to me that morning as he passed my window on his way to work. Now he lay still, the anxiety no longer etched on his face. The Coroner's Officer waited quietly while Anne identified Steve. He was as surprised as I was at her comment "He looks so much younger — he looks almost handsome!"

One has to feel very secure with one's company and the situation to risk making comments in response. Either that or I was just foolhardy. I said "I can just imagine Steve saying 'Anne, you old bat, this is the first time you've ever called me handsome.' "

She laughed. The Coroner's Officer recovered his jaw from the floor and the atmosphere became less tense. Anne was taken home. The paramedic crew sought me out and explained that, in order to reach Steve they had had to up-end the bed. This had the effect of tearing the bedroom light and ceiling rose away from the wiring. Could I, they asked, look in on Anne later that day and rewire the light.

When I called round that evening Anne and other neighbours were sitting round a lit candle—all the house lights having fused. I managed to rewire the bedroom light, replace the fuse in the consumer board, and restore the power. There had been something very gentle about the candle flame. Now the bright electric light revealed the sorrow and tiredness in everyone's faces.

Some weeks later Anne had invited me round for a meal. I arrived as she was finishing the preparation. She looked in the refrigerator for the sunflower margarine and was puzzled that it seemed to be missing. I had a look—indeed I recall squatting down so as to get a clearer view of each shelf. No margarine. We looked on the dining table and on all the worktops. No sign of it. Rather than let it become a problem I volunteered to go home and get mine. I returned less than a minute later. Anne used my supply and reached down to put it in the refrigerator. There was her own tub of margarine. She called me into the kitchen to witness her discovery. I accept that during my absence she might have found her own but, in order to save me embarrassment, had used mine. However the total astonishment on her face belied such a scenario. The margarine had been missing but had now reappeared. We agreed that it was just the kind of light-hearted prank Steve would have played, and we ate our supper reflecting on the possibility that he might, even now, have been around and enjoying the joke.

Some months later I arrived at work to find that a note had been put under my office door by the deputy head porter. "Would it be possible for you to contact the night staff on [he named the ward] this evening as, for the past two nights, they have been having odd occurrences—lights coming on and off, footsteps, patients reporting seeing a nurse in a brown checked uniform, bedpans moving position, TV turning itself on. This is now worrying the staff and they requested help." He signed and dated the note.

One person could have decided to play a game with her or his colleagues during a night shift. Two people might have colluded to make their prank seem more plausible. But for the ward staff as a whole to get to the point of reporting their concern to the person in charge of security and to the chaplain, when this was bound to involve interrogation and investigation, must have meant that they were indeed worried. When my other duties allowed time that morning I called by on the ward and casually checked with the senior nurse the names of the staff who had been on duty the previous night. All but one were due on again the following night. I neither gave nor received any clue that anything was awry. That night I left it until I reckoned that the patients would have settled down before calling to see the staff. I proved that it was impossible to open the door from the corridor on to the ward without making any noise. Although not loud, the squeak and click of the hinges and self closing springs on the door could be heard from the nurses' station when all else was quiet. I had not taken more than a couple of steps into the ward before the entire complement of nurses leapt into view from wherever they had been. I had tried to prepare myself for this visit by considering all the options I could imagine. The attitudes of the staff, their mannerisms, tones of voice—everything needed to be registered in order to build up a reliable picture. It was their universal relief at my presence, their readiness to admit, not only that they were worried, but that they were frightened, which came across to me that night. I do not even recall that they were embarrassed at the incidents they were describing. It cannot have mattered to them whether I thought they were off their trolleys. What they needed was someone who would take them seriously and help them make sense of what was happening so that they could get on with looking after their patients. Their list of events during the previous two nights included the following:

1) Lights turned themselves on twice.
2) Two patients asked to be taken off bedpans which "the nurse" had put them on (neither of them had been put on bedpans).
3) The bedpan from the chair in one area seemed to have disappeared.
4) A fan began oscillating on its own.
5) Footsteps were heard along the corridor, but no-one arrived.
6) The taps in the sluice would start running fast for no apparent reason.
7) A clipboard was found on the floor some distance from the bed to which it belonged.
8) A patient admitted to being frightened but did not know why.
9) Another patient insisted that someone had told her to call a nurse although all the other patients in the area were asleep.

I could produce mundane explanations for most of these "events", and so could the staff on the ward. It is possible that, once sensitised, one could ascribe a significance to such a catalogue of happenings which, in other circumstances, one might have ignored. I began by suggesting that we take practical steps to eliminate the factors we could. Requisitions were filled in for the relevant lights and switches to be checked, for tap washers in the sluice to be replaced, and for the fan to be serviced.

Once I realized that other staff on the ward had been aware of strange happenings I saw the need for containment. If the stories reached the press not only would there be unwelcome visits to the ward by the inquisitive and prurient, disrupting proper functioning, but—and this I saw as even more serious—the patients themselves could become frightened. I felt that we must find a mechanism to enable the staff to report incidents without breach of confidence or accusation of hysteria. I left the ward in the small hours with the piece of paper on which the staff had listed the events I have just quoted.

Two mornings later the ward sister bleeped me. I went straight to the ward to find her in her office with a ward clerk and a student nurse, both as white as sheets and clearly scared out of their wits. The ward clerk had heard water running in the sluice. She and the student nurse had gone to investigate when a stainless steel bedpan had become dislodged from its metal rack and had crashed to the ground at their feet. We had now reached the point when ward staff other than trained nurses were being affected. After consultation with the ward sister I suggested that we briefed all staff on the ward, including junior doctors and the physiotherapists, that there had been reports of unexplained events. So as to minimise the possibility that such events were being contrived by one or two individuals I suggested that there be kept in Sister's office a clipboard to which all ward staff would have access. On it anyone may write a journal report of any incident that troubled them. By appending their name, time, and date they enabled others to corroborate their experience. I asked that such events should not be discussed with anyone other than ward staff. Student nurses were, with full approval, given the home telephone numbers of trained staff so that, if they needed to talk about their experiences, they could do so safely and without involving other students in the School of Nursing.

The first entry on the clipboard was retrospective. Two weeks earlier a staff nurse had found the television set on at 6am in an empty side room. She had cleaned the room and turned everything off the previous evening. Her report concluded:

"? someone watched TV in break." The next night she returned to the ward at 10.30pm after collecting some medicines from another ward and noticed that the television was on again in the same side room. "(Mentioned to staff)". An hour later she "went to kitchen, saw light coming from room #. TV on again. (asked other staff if playing jokes — apparently not). Took other staff to see me unplug TV, lights, shut windows, check loo and shut loo door. 0200hrs approx. Aux. Wallis came down to nurses station stating that TV was on yet again and pulled out from wall. At 0300hrs decided to 'tape' door using 3" tape. 0600hrs tape found neatly rolled back on itself to just over the opening of the door. Nothing inside room touched. Tape re-applied — double! 0730hrs Tape still intact."

8th June

0600   television on in room B.
(cleaned room & turned
everything off previous evening)
? some one watched T.V in
break.

9th June

10.30pm Coming back on ward having
been to C6 to collect some
drugs, noticed T.V. in room
B to be on again.
(mentioned to staff)

1130 pm Went to kitchen, saw light
coming from room B, T.V. on
again.
(Asked other staff if playing
jokes – apparently not.)
Took other staff to see me
unplug T.V. lights, shut
windows, check loo & shut
loo door.

9th June cont...

0200 approx
Aux. Wallis came down to nurses
station stating that T.V. was on
yet again & pulled out from
wall.

at 0300 decided to "tape" door
using 3" tape,

0600 tape found to be neatly rolled
back on itself to just over the
opening of the door. Nothing inside
room touched.
Tape re-applied – double!

0730 tape still intact.

The next page described an incident during the night following my invitation to the ward staff to keep a journal. The nursing auxiliary wrote that the enrolled nurse and he had turned a named patient on to his side. When they returned a couple of hours later he was turned the opposite way round and the pillows had been neatly arranged. I saw the patient the next day and am satisfied that, with his degree of immobility, he could not have rolled himself over, let alone arrange pillows behind his back. The same nursing auxiliary went on to describe how another patient was engaged in deep and serious discussion with someone, although he appeared to be asleep. Unlike his usual ramblings this was "clear cut talk."

The following night there were two pages of notes added to the clipboard. They were initialled by different members of staff but related to the same incidents. At 0400hrs a patient was found to have been incontinent and she was cleaned up. Normally a clear plastic draw sheet was placed above the mattress and underneath the linen draw sheet. For some reason there were no clear plastic draw sheets available and so a white plastic one was used. The nursing auxiliary went to check the patient an hour later to find that she was now lying on a clear plastic draw sheet and that the linen draw sheet had also been changed. The white plastic sheet had been neatly folded up and left on the bedside locker. "This had not been done by any of the three staff on duty." Even without the relevant formal training I could see that such a manoeuvre as changing a draw sheet under so large and immobile a patient would require at least two and preferably three people. As I had demonstrated five nights earlier, it was not possible to sneak on to the ward undetected. In any case, the staff were by now in such a heightened state of awareness that I reckon they would have intercepted intruders and possibly even done them a mischief for causing so much trouble.

From 0600hrs that night the staff and at least one patient heard sounds like "the glugging of a sink." No-one could locate the source of this noise. At 0630hrs a box of tissues was found perched on top of a traction frame. Given that none of the patients was mobile enough to have put it there we were left with two alternatives. Either the occupant of the bed had been a Hoop-la champion or it had been placed there by a member of staff. Partly as an experiment and partly to ease the increasing tension I carried out a study of whether it was possible from within a bed to project a box of tissues up into the air so that, upon its descent, it would land and stay on a traction frame above the bed. The problem was that, in addition to the vertical movement there had to be some horizontal component so that the box, having ascended beside the static traction frame, came down on to it. This horizontal part of the trajectory caused the box to fall off every time. There was much hilarity as nurses, ward clerks, physiotherapist, rugby playing doctors, and I all took turns on the bed (one at a time).

The following night an enrolled nurse noticed "when I was doing the 2200hrs drug round that a patient did not have a drinking glass. The other two staff were unaware of this and when I went back to take a glass there was already one there, filled with water, and had a straw in it." An hour later staff from another ward returned a set of Allen keys (used for adjusting traction frames). The enrolled nurse put them in the drawer in Sister's office. Two hours later, after a search, they were found in the ward clerk's desk drawer. Meanwhile, at 0130hrs, the same nurse was sitting in Sister's office attending to paperwork when the nursing auxiliary entered to find that a Zimmer frame, missing from a patient's bedside, was located behind the chair on which the nurse was sitting. "This frame was *not* in the office when I went in," she wrote. The auxiliary noted that some areas of the ward became suddenly hot and others tremendously cool.

The next entry in the journal was three days later. At 0100hrs the patient in a single room rang his buzzer. He said he felt uneasy, was unable to sleep, and wanted the door left wide open so that "At least I can see if staff walk past." Half an hour later the same member of staff logged that, on going to attend to a patient in another area of the ward, she noticed that there was a used paper cup (such as were used for patients' tea and coffee) upright in the middle of the floor. She noted that she picked it up and put it in the bin. At 0310hrs she noted that on passing the same area "paper cup again, upright, in middle of floor. No staff dropped any cups/touched any cups etc. All patients asleep." My own research into throwing paper cups has produced not one occasion on which they end upright on the floor.

Two nights later the staff nurse in charge made the following entry: "0130 Agency aux. nurse on break (off ward). Agency staff nurse in bay #. I was unpacking Pharmacy box, heard what sounded like Mediscus bed being moved, i.e. buttons being used to alter bed. Went to 'investigate'. Bed found to be different i.e. top and bottom of bed elevated and patient bent double in middle (if you see what I mean!). Control panel on floor *under* bed. (Previously clipped onto cot side) Patient v. distressed.

0300hrs Buzzer went off in room # — patient on weekend leave! Rest of room as left earlier i.e. loo door and window shut — *all* plugs out of socket, call bell on bed.

0400hrs Agency staff nurse on break sat in office reading. Window shut earlier as room draughty. Came out and said the room temperature had *suddenly* dropped and become very cold. When we went back in room did not feel cold, if anything, quite warm. 'Reassured' that it was probably the air conditioning.

0400hrs Agency auxiliary nurse went to answer buzzer in # as light *was* on. No-one had buzzed (no lights on above beds). Patient in bed 12 did ask for extra blanket because she was cold but when asked if she had buzzed said she hadn't. When aux. came out red light above door was off. (swears blind that the light was on before she went in)."

0130   agency aux. nurse on break (off ward)
       agency staff nurse in bay F, I was
       unpacking pharmacy box, heard
       what sounded like mediscus bed
       being moved ie buttons being
       used to alter bed. went to
       "investigate". Bed found to be
       different ie top and ~~bed~~ bottom
       of bed elevated and patient
       bent double in middle
       (~~&~~ if you see what I mean!)
       control panel on floor under
       bed. (previously clipped onto
       cot side) Patient v. distressed.

0300   buzzer went off in room A -
       patient on weekend leave!
       Rest of room as left earlier
       ie loo door & window shut -
       all plugs out of socket, call
       bell on bed.

~~........~~ Agency staff nurse on break sat
             in office reading. Window shut
0400   earlier as room draughty. Came
*   out as said the room
PTD   temperature had suddenly

dropped and become very cold, when
we went back in room did not feel
cold, if anything, quite warm,
"Reassured" that it was probably the
air conditioning!

0400 Agency aux. nurse went to answer
     * buzzer in E as light was on.
TWO
INCIDENTS No one had buzzed (no lights on
SAME !! above beds)
TIME
       Patient in bed 12 did ask for
       extra blanket because she was
       cold but when asked if she
       had buzzed said she hadn't.
       When aux. came out red light
       above door was off
       (swears blind that the light was
       on before she went in)

These incidents involved agency staff who had no prior briefing about the ward's events. At the time there was no air conditioning on the ward and the hospital's engineer assured me that the computer log of the ward's temperature showed no glitches that night. When patients "buzzed" they pressed a button on a small panel which was usually within reach on the bed. A cable connected it to the wall. When this Nurse Call system was activated lights at the bed head, outside the room, and at the nurses station all came on and stayed on until cancelled by the pressing of another button at the bed head In addition there was in intermittent sounder providing an audible as well as visible alarm. The agency auxiliary would not have known to go to a particular area unless that area's red light had come on above the door. Having entered the room she would expect to find a further red light at the bed head of the patient who had "buzzed." It looks as if the system had somehow been cancelled between her entering the room and completing her search of the beds. My own experience indicated that you needed to be more agile than most of those patients to be able to reach behind and above the bed to press the "Cancel" button from within the bed.

The next night at 0140hrs the staff nurse had gone to the sluice for a draw sheet, passing the open door of a single room. After completing her task back at a patient's bed she was returning to the sluice just as I entered the ward at the other end of the corridor. She waved, took a couple of steps towards the sluice, stopped and turned, staring and pointing into the single room which she had passed between three and five minutes earlier. The television set in that room was now on, which it had not been earlier. Either that staff nurse had the potential for a talented career on the stage or she was genuinely witness, as was I, to yet another "happening."

Two nights later at 0325hrs the staff nurse went into Sister's office to start compiling the Pharmacy order. She noted that the desk chair was in an unusual position in front of the refrigerator, facing out of the office. She spoke with all the staff. None of them had moved any chairs, and it was definitely not there at midnight as her colleague would have had to climb round it to get medicines out of the refrigerator.

Three nights later I visited the ward at 0025hrs. On the way past the kitchen I glanced in as the lights were on, but there was no-one there. The staff were together at the nurses' station and we chatted for about twenty minutes. During that time we heard no-one enter or leave the ward, and none of the patients was mobile enough to have got up out of bed unaided. As I left I heard the sound of running water from the kitchen. I went in to find, not water, but milk pouring from the refrigerated milk container into the drip tray below. I just managed to operate the tap before the tray overflowed. I returned swiftly (we are not supposed to run) to the nurses station and the staff came back to the kitchen with me to watch me carry the perilously full drip tray to the sink. Only as I poured it away did we notice that there was a rancid smell. The milk was "off." None of the staff had been to the kitchen for over an hour. They had used milk from the ordinary refrigerator, not the machine. I cannot remember who said it, but I was struck that this was the first time that any of the staff had ascribed any of these "happenings" to a person. "I wouldn't have smelt that milk before giving it to a patient. She must have been trying to tell us something. She was trying to help." I had been scrupulous not to "give a lead" as to who or what, if anything, was behind these events.

During the next eleven weeks there were further reports of strange sounds from the sluice, bedpans being re-arranged, doors opening and shutting, lights being turned off unaided, a wheelchair suddenly appearing behind a nurse who was seated at the nurses' station, trapping her. Four months after the first reported "happening" the senior staff nurse and a student nurse heard someone talking to them at 0250hrs near the nurses' station. No patients were nearby. The third member of staff, the nursing auxiliary, was out of earshot checking patients. Later that night the staff found that the curtains had been drawn round the beds of two patients. "None of us left the areas like that as we all worked together" when turning patients. Ten days later the ward clerk rang my office asking if I would be free that afternoon to visit the ward. I did so to hear that the previous night two of the regular nursing staff had simultaneously heard a young woman scream. Unsolicited they were then assured by a patient who had presumably also heard it that "It wasn't me screaming." There were no patients or staff on the ward that night likely to have been the source of the scream. My enquiries of adjacent wards also drew a blank.

Not long after this the ward closed for redecoration. The staff and patients were transferred and no further "happenings" were reported by the new occupants of the ward when it re-opened some months later, with different staff and patients. The ward sister brought the clip board and the journal to my office for safe keeping. Who or what, she asked, did I think was behind everything. I explained that I had been building up a picture of a nurse who loved her work and her patients who had died suddenly—so suddenly that, bizarre as it may sound, she had not realized that her life's work was finished. Although I already knew the answer I asked the ward sister if any nurses or nursing auxiliaries of her acquaintance had died in the last year or so. One had, and we discovered that her last shift had been a night on that ward. The scream had been on the first anniversary of her death, although she had died in her sleep.

The ward sister, for whom I have an abiding high regard, felt that any formal "service" of exorcism or release would trap her staff in assumptions with which some would be uncomfortable. Would it be sufficient, she asked, if I could find some way on my own of helping her erstwhile colleague go free.

Compiling this chapter, reflecting on her care for the patients, her mischievous practical jokes on her colleagues, her use of me to deal with the rancid milk, combined with my recollection of her as she lay in the chapel of rest when I took her family to see her — all of this led to the most natural of affectionate thoughts "Go to your rest with our love. Thank you for your help, your care, and your fun. Go well."

True religion

What did the flight attendant do when the airline pilot said he was about to ditch and suggested she encourage the passengers to do something religious? She took a collection!

The words "religion" and "religious" are powerfully emotive, but their meaning is as variable as their use.

Following a miscarriage a couple in the Delivery Unit asked their midwife what would happen to their baby. She replied that she had a colleague who deals with this kind of thing.

"Who?" asked the young man.

"One of our chaplains," replied the midwife.

With horror he said "But we're not religious."

"Ha!" was the response. "You ought to see our chaplains, they're not religious either!"

Some people consider her remark impertinent if not offensive. If there is one thing clergy ought to be, they argue, it is religious. But what does that mean? Many see clergy as killjoys, hypocrites, windbags, control freaks, or harbingers of death, doom, and disaster. Others see them as a parasitic irrelevance to real life. Some people base these perceptions on painful or embarrassing past experience of encounters with clergy, ministers of religion, or characters presumed to be religious. For others it is convenient to ridicule and marginalise those whose philosophy they secretly admire but lack the courage to follow. Maybe my own experience of school made me sensitive to my colleagues' descriptions of their school-days. Nurses in particular spoke with bitterness of the vicious treatment some of them had received at the hands of nuns at convent schools—supposedly in the name of religion "for the good of their souls."

Whatever else was required of me it was essential that I was not to be "religious" with this couple. The midwife introduced me to them as "Ian". This, I discovered later, surprised them since they presumed that people wearing clerical collars required greater formality. I invited them to give me some idea of how they wanted to handle the leave-taking from their baby. The options included burial or cremation, with or without their involvement, as they wished. They could get in touch with a funeral director or, if they did not want to involve anyone else, I was prepared to act as undertaker. Burial in their village cemetery appealed, as did the idea that I tuck their baby up in a tiny white coffin, fix a nameplate on the lid, and take him to the cemetery, having arranged for the digging of the grave. I explained that normally I travelled on a motorcycle but that on this occasion, out of respect, I would bring the coffin in a car. The young man's eyes opened wide with surprise.

"You ride a bike? I want any son of mine to have a ride on a bike. You bring him on your bike!"

So I did. On arrival at the cemetery he lifted the coffin out of the top box of my motorcycle and carried it tenderly to the graveside where, without any words, we knelt on the grass in order to place their babe in his resting place. We were to return to the cemetery some weeks later.

It is less easy than people imagine to determine the sex of a miscarried foetus by external looks alone. In this case it was only when the parents returned to the hospital to discuss the findings of the post-mortem examination that they discovered that their baby was a girl. The mother ran, crying, from the clinic, through the hospital, to my office. It would have been unhelpful for me to have reminded her that the midwife had said that their baby was *probably* a boy but that it was difficult to be sure at such an early stage of gestation. Instead I invited them both (for her husband, guessing that she had made for my office, had now caught up with her) to consider how they wanted to put the record straight. It was largely a matter of getting their heads round a different set of assumptions about their baby. Most tangible was that she had the wrong name. This became the focus for their attention. The nameplate on her coffin was wrong. I assured them that this could be changed. A new nameplate was made and the grave was re-opened very carefully. Sitting on the edge with my feet in the grave beside the coffin, I removed the existing nameplate and replaced it with the new one. The symbolic correction made, I mused on the idea that their little girl might have been laughing at us all the time for taking so long to catch up with who she was, even to the extent of defining her as a "girl biker". This clearly appealed to her parents.

When her younger sister was born I had the privilege of being her first visitor—within 20 minutes of her arrival. Some five years later her mother brought her to see me. She recognised me from a photograph taken when she was three months old, of me holding her in my arms after christening her in her local parish church. I was immediately accepted by her, even to the extent of being required, at the end of their visit, to give her a "piggy-back" from the front entrance of the hospital to the car park.

In response to a bleep message I rang a midwife on the Delivery Unit. She wanted the telephone number of a Muslim priest. I explained that there were different denominations within Islam, as there were within the Christian religion. It could be embarrassing, if not distressing, were I to produce the wrong one. My offer to go to the Unit and find out what was required was readily accepted. As I stepped into a lift I was greeted with "Christ! Not you!"

I looked at the other occupant, a total stranger, with a mixture of surprise and puzzlement.

"No, no" I replied. "I'm just his very junior assistant."

Did the man perceive me as the Grim Reaper? I am not particularly skeletal or cadaverous, and I do not own a scythe. Had he seen me wearing a halo or, more likely, a crown of thorns? If so I was unaware of such an honour. Did he think that, because I was a "clerge" I had some second sight into his murky past? Or was I some sort of Jonah, who would cause the lift's steel ropes to snap and send us crashing to our deaths at the bottom of the lift shaft? I suspect that my reply to his exclamation took him time to digest, and I alighted with no further comment.

Within the Delivery Unit I was introduced to a young Arab man whose first-born child, a son, had just been delivered. He was dead. I apologised for my intrusion and explained my desire to ensure that we obtain the right person for him.

"You are a holy man," he said. "We both believe in God. You call him God. I call him Allah. We are both men of the book. I read the Koran. You read the Bible. I think your Jesus Christ was a very great prophet."

"So we are fellow travellers?" I responded tentatively.

"Yes," he said. "You're travelling by National Express, and I'm on foot!"

"I won't have that," I replied smiling. "Pray Allah we both arrive safely."

"Please will you come and pray for my son?"

For me the challenge was not in whispering into his baby's ear the prayer "God is great", but in the contrast between this encounter and that in the lift half an hour earlier. Then there had been fear, hostility, possibly superstition. Now there was welcome, tolerance, and an acceptance of reality. While for many Western sophisticates religion is used as a mechanism for escaping from reality, here was a couple to all appearances accepting the harshest of realities, and inviting me to give expression to their spirituality. I left the Delivery Unit wondering who had been ministering to whom.

It was late one Friday evening when the consultant in charge of the Neonatal Intensive Care Unit rang me. "Are you any good at being an Orthodox Jewish rabbi?" My answer that I would probably be useless was irrelevant since it was clear that the staff on the Unit wanted some moral support even if the Jewish couple in question found me unacceptable. On arrival I was briefed about a very premature baby who had been clinging precariously on to life for some days. As so often, as I had been told, the blood vessels around and within the brain were so fragile and underdeveloped that the strain of independent existence had been too much and blood had leaked into the brain cells, destroying them. His parents would have liked to have the support of their own rabbi at such a time, but they knew that once the Sabbath had begun at sunset on Friday he would not answer his telephone or drive to the hospital. Instead they accepted me as a stranger to sit with them as they cuddled their baby for the first time since his birth. Until now, while there was any possibility of his survival, he had lain in an incubator, his breathing being done for him by a special fast-oscillating ventilator. Now the priority was that they have all the time available to treasure him. Their tradition required that when Jewish men prayed they covered their heads. Out of respect I found and donned a theatre cap. Together we sat and, at their invitation, I held a lighted candle as I recited one of the Psalms of David. It had been 35 years since I had attempted to study Hebrew, and so I was grateful that they allowed me to recite Psalm 23 in English. The ventilator was turned off when they were ready, and for the next two hours we kept their little Adam warm against our bodies. Eventually the consultant could detect no heartbeat. The remaining tubes were removed and, with the support of a nurse, the parents washed and dressed him as I knelt on the floor beside them. With a look that would brook no opposition, the father said "Will you please carry him to the mortuary? We trust you."

Ten days later the parents sent me a card with a gold Star of David on the front, thanking me for helping them. Some 13 months after that I received a bleep call informing me that someone was waiting to see me in the hospital chapel. On arrival I recognised Adam's father.

"Simon," I said. "What brings you here?"

"We have a new son, Benjamin. You must come and meet him!"

It was after a nine-year-old had died on the operating table that I took his mother to the chapel of rest to say goodbye. Since she was a Hindu I had removed all symbols of the Christian religion from the chapel. Afterwards as we walked down to the hospital car park the mother suddenly stopped, turned to me, and said "You must have to face this often. What do you think happens when we die?"

I begged her to bear with me if my Western Christian culture was alien to her. But she interrupted me "I believe in God," she said. "What do you think happens when we die?"

"I believe in a God who is big enough, and good enough, and loving enough to take care of those we love, even when they pass beyond our care in death, and to keep them safe with him until we are allowed to join them in Heaven."

"Good," she replied. "So if I ask you to pray for my son you'll know what to do, and you'll do it, won't you!"

A train crash or other accident which places demands on the Emergency Services beyond their normal capacity is generally declared to be a Major Incident. The local police force recognised that there could be situations where there were large numbers of victims trapped by wreckage or awaiting removal from the scene of the accident. Police, fire, and ambulance staff would, by definition, be stretched to their limits using their skills in removing the trapped and injured. I was asked to help train clergy, ministers, and other representatives of Christian denominations, so that they could provide companionship and containment to victims awaiting extrication or removal from the scene. They were not expected to engage in heroics, but rather to act under the direction of Emergency Service personnel, staying with the injured or trapped to let them know that they had not been forgotten, until skilled staff could attend to them. In respect of the walking victims awaiting removal from the scene their role was to prevent the "headless chicken" syndrome — to stay with the shocked, discouraging them from running back into the carnage to retrieve, for instance, their luggage.

Local church leaders nominated clergy and others whom they considered might be appropriate for training, and the police force set up a course for them. My task was to prepare them for the emotional, psychological, and spiritual demands that might be made upon them. I began by asking them to divide up into pairs, preferably with someone they did not know. I then asked them each to spend two minutes describing to the other the most traumatic experience of their life. I would not be requiring them to report on their experience and so it could remain confidential between them. One or two participants subsequently told me that they had been surprised how shaken they had been by recalling the incidents they had.

I then asked them, staying in their pairs, to describe to each other what, in human terms, they had found most helpful in their traumatic experience. At the end of quarter of an hour I drew their recollections to a close and gave them a few moments to disengage from them. Having reminded them that the experiences could remain confidential if they wished I invited everyone to report what it was, in human terms, that they had found most helpful within the experience. The holding of a hand, an arm round a shoulder, sitting or weeping quietly together—these were the most reported responses. One man told us of an incident in which he had been stabbed in the neck. While some people restrained his attacker one person sat on the ground, "cradling my head in his arms, so that he could apply pressure to my neck to limit the bleeding—and he was an Asian Muslim."

At the end of about an hour of feedback I drew together the common features of what the volunteers had found most helpful. After all, it was those same factors which their victims were likely to appreciate in them. I noticed a broad grin forming on the face of the police sergeant hosting the meeting. He could see where I was leading before I delivered the *coup de grâce*.

"You are priests, clergy, ministers, pastors, elders of the Christian faith. Not one of you has included in your list of what in human terms *you* found most helpful, reading the Bible, praying, confession, anointing, or communion. Statistically it is therefore pretty unlikely that such activities will be required of you at the scene of a Major Incident by others, even though, in the light of Church teaching, you might have imagined they would."

They themselves had not needed "churchy" or "religious" activities in the traditional sense. One or two of the participants withdrew from the call-out list, because "blood and guts" were not their scene. I suspect that others declined further involvement because they needed to be *doing* something, and my exercise had demonstrated that the kind of things they wanted to do were not in demand, even by them when they were traumatised.

Within our own hospital we had occasion to activate our own Major Incident response. Chlorine gas had escaped from the plant room adjacent to the hydrotherapy pool. Staff and patients in adjoining areas were overcome and brought up to our Accident and Emergency Department. Their normal clothes, reeking of chlorine, were removed and they all put on theatre "greens". They were sitting together awaiting individual assessment and attention. As part of the Major Incident response the Chaplaincy was notified, and I attended. Having been briefed by the consultant in charge I stood casually in the doorway of the room in which the 20 or 30 people were sitting coughing.

"What the hell are you doing here?" enquired one member of staff.

"I'm responding to a Major Incident and assessing whether there is any case for my involvement."

"You mean this is being treated as a Major Incident?"

I was the first evidence that it was. In spite of the potentially fatal circumstances it was amusing to watch the change in everyone's demeanour following this realisation. They were being treated seriously. This was not regarded as a hysterical response to a nasty smell. I sensed that I was permitted to move further into the room and to sit down with them. We chatted about how cleaning the loo at home or taking the children swimming might, in the future, trigger uncomfortable associations with today. There was laughter that this provided a novel excuse for someone else to carry out these duties for once!

This was not an occasion for holding the hands of the trapped or shocked, but one for being their companion, letting them know that they were still special by simply being with them in their experience. The nearest we got to "religious" language was the following day when I telephoned the homes of everyone who had been involved. "Bless you for ringing" was the response from several of those who had suddenly been turned into victims the previous day.

All too often funerals are "religious" in the very worst sense. You submit yourself to formal clothing, to a building and music you normally avoid, to allowing a stranger with a set of alien presuppositions to speak of someone he has never met, but whom you have known well, possibly loved, and all of this in 25 minutes while you are struggling with profound emotions and issues of "Where is she now? Does she know my heart is breaking?" The worst criticism I heard of someone conducting a funeral was from a mourner who said "We weren't even sure that we were at the right service."

I had been asked to conduct the funeral of a police officer. His death had been sudden, but was due to natural causes. The crematorium chapel was packed with colleagues of all ranks, standing stiffly where there was no room to sit, all in uniform. His colleagues from the police Underwater Unit, of which he had been a member, were to carry his coffin into the chapel. Knowing that he had loved water sports I arranged with the organist to play us in to "Stormy Weather." Having led the little procession bearing the coffin in to the chapel I took my place and the music stopped. The expectation was that I would read some passages from the Bible. Instead I said "I know and you know what a private person Tom has been—how acutely embarrassed he'd be at the sight of us lot here on his account. I have a mental picture of him looking in through the doors you've just come in by, and seeing all of us here, he says "Stuff this for a lark! I'm going windsurfing!"

It was not just the chuckle of recognition that I noted. I reckon that at least thirty people glanced round at the doors to see if Tom was there.

Colleagues paid tribute to him, music was played, and I had to find words which avoided the knee-jerk reaction of antagonism to "religious" language.

"We remember with thanks all that Tom has meant to us, all that he has been for us, all that he has made of us, and all that he has left with us. We hold in the arms of our thoughts all those who love him, all those who miss him, all those who grieve for him. In a moment of silence we express our hope that he may be at peace with the world, with his maker, and with himself."

As people filed out of the chapel after the funeral one police sergeant collared me. "I'm not religious—not at all religious. But that was the most spiritual service I've ever been at."

Shortly before eight o'clock one evening I was at home when my daughter rang. As part of her degree course she was required to lead a seminar the following morning on "Religion." "Help!"

I suggested that she begin with a definition. That way there was an objective basis for discussion. So far as I knew, I explained, throughout the Jewish Scriptures (the Old Testament) and the Christian books of the New Testament there is one definition of religion.

"Right. Quote!" she demanded.

"'True religion is to care for the widow and fatherless in their distress and to keep yourself unstained by the world.'"

"Wow!" she exclaimed. "No mention of going to church!"

At that moment my bleep went off. Normally the voice message is a request to ring a telephone number, generally an extension within the hospital. This message was different: "Ian. It's Accident Service. We need you. Quick!"

My daughter heard this over the telephone and we agreed to end the conversation. I told her where to find the passage I had quoted (Letter of James, chapter 1, verse 27). I suggested that she call me again at 7.30 the next morning, which would still be at the cheap rate, and we rang off. I rang Accident Service and then went straight in to the Department. I returned home at 4.30am. and was woken three hours later by the telephone.

"That quotation was brilliant. I think I've got enough material for the seminar. Incidentally, what were you called in for?"

"I was called in to support someone whose husband had been struggling with alcoholism for years. He thought he had beaten it, but last night he realised that it had beaten him. He and his wife had been sitting on the edge of their bed. While she reached across to the dressing table for some tissues he reached under the bed for a gun and shot himself. I spent most of last night sharing the silence with her and her 21-year-old fatherless son."

Bad news

On the noticeboard beside the nurses' station on a ward of my acquaintance there is a cartoon strip. The first picture is of a ward sister wearing the now rarely seen frilly uniform cap and sleeves, and possessed of the typical caricature of a hatchet face. She is addressing appropriately subdued student nurses: "There are two main sources of infection." The next picture is of her pointing at a lavatory bowl and saying "lavatory pans..." The third picture is of her pointing with contempt at a young man wearing a white coat, adding "... and medical students."

As a generalisation the cartoon may nowadays be unfair, but old prejudices persist. Medical or, as they are now called, clinical students are, in my experience, highly intelligent, highly motivated, ambitious, competitive, and keenly aware of who holds the key to their future promotion. Many are also thoughtful and humane. They soak up facts and regurgitate them in examinations. The development of the "bedside manner" comes later, sometimes very much later. But few of them have experienced first hand the crushing effect of unremitting pain, other than in hangovers. Not many people in general in their early twenties have been touched by life limiting illnesses or the death of those near to them. This is why the Postgraduate Dean of the Clinical School asked me to run seminars for his students on "Breaking Bad News."

Some students would, on arrival, look round the lecture room for charts, overhead or slide projectors, X-ray viewing boxes — the aids to absorbing more facts. Others, concluding that I did not look as interesting as the dissecting aortic aneurysm they had been invited to watch being repaired, took one look and left for the operating theatre. Occasionally I detected the truculence of unwilling students.

In such cases I would start the seminar with "Why do you want to be doctors? You don't look like masochists, but do you not realize that in Great Britain at present we are confronted with a 100% mortality rate" (and they would write this down!). "You can put your hand on your heart or indeed, with some force, on your patient's heart, and say 'My life is going to be a total failure because every one of my patients is going to die either because of me or in spite of me. And then I'm going to die'. Now, why the hell do you want to be doctors?"

I suspect that they had never been confronted with such a question, certainly not one presented like this. It was generally followed by another question. "Why do we so dread breaking bad news to people — whether about their own condition or that of someone dear to them?" Typical answers were:

i) It causes pain both to them and us, and

ii) It appears to be in breach of the Hippocratic principle "Do no harm." At first sight the dilemma for the doctor appears to be "Should I tell or not?" I try to extend the issue to "When and how should I tell someone that their life expectancy is limited or that, say, their parent has died?"

I was sitting with a woman whose husband was undergoing surgery. There were only the two of us in the room adjoining the Intensive Care Unit when the surgeon came in. He was wearing theatre "greens" and he still had on his white surgeon's boots which were splattered with blood. With wide-eyed panic he scanned the small room. As if willing there to be no one of the patient's name present he said "Mrs A?"

I pointed to her. He hung on to the door handle as if on a bus that was about to leave without him.

"I'm Mr B. I have been operating on your husband." One out of ten for introducing himself. "The anastomosis worked very well. However, we had considerable difficulty achieving haemostasis." I looked at his boots and thought "That is an understatement.'"

"Regrettably he has succumbed." And the surgeon left.

Mrs A turned to me and said "Can I go and see Jack?"

Quietly I replied that I thought Mr B was trying to tell us that Jack had died. In that I could still hear the footsteps of the surgeon as he fled along the corridor I suspect that he, too, could hear her scream as the time bomb he had triggered went off.

For even the most erudite of clinical students "succumbed" is not part of their everyday vocabulary. Some admitted to using the word as a euphemism when one of their colleagues slid off a bar stool in an alcoholic stupor, but the general consensus was that it was better to use everyday language.

I was interested by the students' thoughts about the terms "Jack is dead" and "Jack has died." The first was felt to be more direct: "This is how Jack is." It was preferred by students with a distaste for unnecessary chatter; "get in, get to the point, and get out." On the other hand "Jack has died" had a gentler sound. It was thought to imply that he was more involved in the process, more in charge of his destiny. It was suggested that such an interpretation might cause grieving relatives to become angry with the dead person for having deserted them. The contrary view expressed was that, since anger is a common early reaction to news of bereavement (what I refer to as "impotent fury") the choice of words was probably incidental to whether or not anger would be expressed.

I presented the students with another scenario. Vicky's parents knew that she had a very serious abnormality, and that it was life-threatening. As she developed the burden on her system would become unbearable and she would die. The surgeon, Mr C, made it clear that any surgery to which they gave consent was breaking new ground and that Vicky might well die during the operation or soon after it. Sitting on the floor beside them after they had been given this information I remained silent as her parents wept and hugged each other. For 20 minutes I said nothing until her father said "Thanks, Ian. You've helped a lot."

Looking up at him I whispered "How?"

"Just being here. You cared."

Vicky survived the surgery but was desperately weak. In a letter to me after she died (to which I shall refer again later) her mother said she felt no bitterness about what happened, just a great respect for the hospital. "It is a comfort to know that if anyone could have pulled Vicky through Mr C and his team would have done. It was very touching to see the doctors and nurses taking only ten minutes for lunch to be back at Vicky's bedside and to see Mr C prepare to spend the night near her after spending all day in theatre. Our feelings apart, I wish they could have pulled her through. They certainly deserved to."

To be fair, and the students rightly pointed this out, some relatives will not believe such prognoses however well or often they are told. That, we concluded, was no excuse for failing to make the effort. While most of the students stressed the importance of giving hope, whether to the patient himself or to the relatives, some identified the dangers of raising false or unrealistic expectations. They saw, as I have seen, a tendency in the general public in Britain to assume (erroneously) that health is a legal right, and that anyone who has the gall to challenge that assumption should be sued. Previous generations of doctors and patients may have been content to collude with what others have called the paternalism of the medical profession. Nowadays such behaviour in a doctor is in danger of reinforcing the patient's demand that all disease must be cured, or the doctor is deemed to be negligent. For some of the students in these seminars this discussion was far too "touchy-feely." But others, somewhat diffidently, would voice concern that some of their mentors were in danger of "playing God" with their patients, to the detriment of realism and truth. When it comes to telling relatives that the person they have cared for, loved, hated, or been concerned for, has died there is no easy formula. All students agreed that the approach of Mr B was disastrous—but in what ways?

At least he introduced himself and provided evidence that he was competent to give the information about Jack. His clothing clearly gave the message that he had come straight from the operating theatre, but the bloody boots struck the students as unhygienic and insensitive. His choice of language suggested he was trying to hide the reality of Jack's death from both himself and Jack's wife. His hanging on to the door handle, standing as far away from the seated person to whom he was speaking as possible, was another message that he was desperate not to engage in any real communication with her. In summary, he betrayed that he looked on this as a distasteful task he could not avoid but which he would complete with maximum speed and minimum distress to himself.

A few students had experience of being told of the death of people dear to them. Little things seemed significant to them. The doctor, having entered the room and introduced himself or herself, would ask permission to sit down. This gave the message that "this is your territory and I want to tread carefully in it." It also declared that "whatever my professional status, when it comes to the issue in hand we are on equal terms." When there was no question from those in the room like "How is she?" it helped if the doctor broke the ice with something like "May I check with you what you understand of Mrs D's condition?" Not only does this ensure that he is in the right room with the right people, but it also gives them the chance to say how much they know of what has been happening, and how grave they understand her condition to be. It may also help the doctor determine something of the dynamics between the members of the family. One student told me that she knew her friend had died even before the surgeon spoke. She could see it in his face.

Relatives have told me that they found it much more bearable when the doctor sat down with them, explained that despite the very best efforts of the clinical team Mrs D has died, concluding with "I am so sorry." Especially when the doctor or surgeon then stayed sitting silently with the family, they told me it made them realize how hard the team must have worked, how wretched they must have felt, and how glad the family was that, say, their mother had been in the hands of people who cared. By the very act of staying with the relatives the doctor communicates that there is no further clinical intervention appropriate for Mrs D. If the family does not dismiss him with "Thank you, doctor. We'll be all right", it seems as if 90 seconds—interminable as it may feel—is about long enough to convey, by inaction as well as by words, that the struggle is over. Ideally a nurse, chaplain, or other member of staff will be sitting with the relatives and so the doctor can take her or his leave with something like "If you find there's something you want to ask me Nurse can bleep me and I'll do my very best to help."

I generally concluded my seminars in the Clinical School with stark realism. "When you apply for Specialist Registrar training posts [the preparation for becoming consultants] you know that you'll have to produce *curricula vitae* with full details of all the procedures you've carried out, all the research you've done and had published. The selection panel will find it exceedingly difficult to choose the best of a very bright bunch. One factor may sway the panel, and it has nothing to do with your skill with a stethoscope or scalpel. It is this: 'Can we afford to appoint this person? Is his/her way of relating to ill people and their families so inept that they complain and the Hospital Trust is going to be paying out hand over fist in out-of-court settlements?'"

The point is that breaking bad news should not seen as a distasteful part of the job, to be avoided or rushed through. It has dramatic and long-term consequences on the health and well-being of those being given such news. It therefore requires quite as high a level of skill in watchful sensitivity, courtesy, and tact as in any other clinical activities. As will be shown later, to get it right (or at least as far from wrong as possible) at this critical time is to engage in good preventative medicine.

Resuscitation

To fall asleep during a sermon is generally frowned upon (particularly if it is the preacher who nods off). I preferred to think that if a member of the congregation dozed off during my sermon then that person must be feeling relaxed and secure, and that the cat-nap was probably doing them more good than my ramblings.

One Sunday morning I was helping out in a church near the hospital. The vicar who usually covered my duties when I was on holiday was himself away and I was returning the favour. It was during my brief address that I noticed one lady at the back of the church slide quietly off her chair on to the floor.

Her face had turned waxy white. Beads of sweat glistened on her forehead, and her eyes rolled before she disappeared from my view. This, I thought, was not someone falling asleep, but having a heart attack. I looked at my watch, left the pulpit, walked swiftly to where she lay, and put her in the recovery position. Since most of the congregation were seated in front of her they had not seen her collapse and were therefore puzzled by my truncated sermon and unscripted movement to the back of the church.

I tried to find a pulse. One of the things I had not been told in first aid training is how hard it is to locate a pulse when you are under pressure. Neither in her wrist nor in her neck could I find any evidence of heartbeat. I asked someone to call an ambulance, reporting a collapse at the church. Then I moved the chairs out of the way, rolled her on to her back, and started the cardio-pulmonary resuscitation (C.P.R.) I had practised on dummies. The second thing I had not been told was how exhausting this activity was when you had no help. Two full breaths to try to inflate the lungs with oxygenated air followed by 15 compressions on the chest to encourage the heart to pump—this cycle repeated in earnest is tiring. I had been told that if the brain is starved of oxygenated blood for more than three minutes it can suffer irreversible damage. This was a witnessed arrest, and I knew that my time was nearly up when I heard the ambulance siren.

As the paramedics ran up the paved path to the church I felt a flicker of a pulse in the lady's neck. The door burst open and I sat back on my haunches as she came round. The first words spoken since I had called for the ambulance were from the paramedic who shouted "Hey Ian! How the hell did you get here first?" They came swiftly to her, gave her oxygen, applied the electrocardiograph leads, and then put her on their trolley so as to transfer her to our local hospital.

After they had left we straightened up the chairs and I returned to the front of the church. I sat down on the altar steps and asked the congregation to allow me a few minutes to regain my breath. They laughed and clapped. The service continued and our prayers for the sick had an added immediacy. I visited the lady later in the day on the coronary care unit. She made what I was told was a good recovery and was discharged home.

Two contradictory stories circulated in the neighbourhood. The first was that I was a dangerous preacher, causing people to have heart attacks. The second was that, if you were going to have a cardiac arrest, then make sure there's someone nearby who can perform C.P.R.

More recently I have been used by course tutors to present an ethical perspective on resuscitation. First aiders, paramedics, and G.P.s attending road traffic accidents and other emergencies are taught C.P.R. but it has been felt important to give such practitioners an insight into the ethical and medico-legal implications of such a procedure. What I did in that church, in front of 60 or so witnesses, was at least common assault, if not battery or grievous bodily harm. I forced an old lady on to her back on the floor, clapped my mouth over hers, groped around her chest, and, especially if she had been suffering from osteoporosis, could well have cracked a rib or two in the process. This activity, like many other clinical procedures, (including rendering someone unconscious with an anaesthetic), constitutes a serious offence against the person, and has to be justified by actual or presumed consent, and that it is intended to achieve the good of that person. In the heat of the moment you give this no more than a fleeting glance, but even that glance can check you from using, or abusing, the victim as a specimen on which to practise and show off your skills. By definition I could not lift an unconscious eyelid and say "Would you like me to attempt to resuscitate you?" I had to presume that she would have given me permission to try to save her life. There might have been a relative or friend of hers in the congregation who knew that she suffered from a dicky ticker and that she was quite content that her life might end soon. Even if that companion had told me that the lady would rather not be resuscitated I would have been on weaker legal ground had I stopped my attempt than if it had been possible to produce a previously signed statement to that effect. But how many of us carry such documents? A consultant in cardiology at a London hospital told me that he had tattooed across his chest "Do not resuscitate", but I had to take his word for it. He said that if he had a cardiac arrest on the steps of his hospital the first thing he would do if he came round was "get up and run like hell!"

Even when someone has expressed their wishes in writing there is the issue of competence. Did they have a clear understanding   of   what   was   written   and   of   the consequences? Were they under pressure from relatives who stood to benefit from the Will? Were they of a sound mind when they wrote the directive, and have they changed their mind since then? (When I deposited my own draft guidelines or "Value Directive" on the subject with my G.P. he expressed his satisfaction with the content but suggested that I get it checked out for legal clarity. In fact I had had it vetted the previous day by the Professor of Medical Ethics at Oxford University and by the Legal Officer of the General Medical Council. This satisfied my G.P. that the guidelines were legally sound.)

The second principle to be borne in mind when attempting C.P.R. is: "Will the patient be in a worse condition than before if he/she survives the cardiac or respiratory arrest?'" In other words "Is resuscitation in the patient's best interests?"

An elderly man collapsed in the street. An ambulance was called and the crew attempted full C.P.R. both at the scene and in the vehicle all the way to hospital. After a further 30 minutes' effort in the resuscitation room it was concluded that life was extinct. His body was wheeled into a single cubicle and his wife sat grieving beside him. The debris of the attempt to save his life was cleared from the floor of the resuscitation room and the physician in charge rang the coroner's office to report the death. Ten minutes later a long deep groan was heard coming from the cubicle. The crash team who had been about to leave dived into the cubicle, dragged the trolley with the "dead" man on it back into the resuscitation room and started on him again. I understand that they made his heart begin some sort of activity on its own. My brief was to support his wife who had been thrown about on a switchback of emotions — first of adjusting to the fact that he had died, and then that he was alive again.

Even if his heart was beating after a fashion the extended period over which the brain had been starved of oxygen (over 60 minutes) would have caused irreversible damage.

In the event he "survived" on a ward for 35 hours without regaining consciousness. The emotional strain on his wife was enormous, for she had been exposed to medicine at its most grotesque. Needless to say, the coroner was not amused. The pathologist who carried out the coroner's post mortem examination explained to me that the groan was probably the consequence of "agonal reflexes", of nerves responding to the chemical changes following death and causing muscles in the diaphragm to tweak. I was to be thankful for that briefing in a later incident.

The third principle to consider when attempting C.P.R. is this: "Can I reverse the underlying reason for this person's cardiac or respiratory arrest, or am I interrupting the natural process at the end of life?" If choking on a peanut is the cause of the arrest then, after timely removal of the obstruction, resuscitation stands a fair chance of being successful.

It was the last wish of a man with cancer that he be taken from the hospice to watch a cricket match between two local village teams. St John's Ambulance ferried him to the ground and he sat in a wheelchair in front of the pavilion with his family. As the game proceeded he slipped into unconsciousness and died—just where he would have wished. A bystander, unknown to his family, used a mobile telephone to ring for an emergency ambulance. When the paramedics arrived the family had to use all their powers of persuasion to convince them that to attempt C.P.R. was not only futile but undignified, since they were never going to reverse his underlying terminal condition.

The problem for anyone, whether as a professional or as an informed volunteer, when confronted with someone who has collapsed is lack of information. "Have I permission to attempt C.P.R.? Has irreversible brain or other organ damage happened already? Was this a peaceful and natural end-of-life event?" The guidance now widely offered is "Make a start at C.P.R., but be ready to stop if information becomes available which indicates that further efforts are inappropriate."[2] This is easier said than done. The popular perception is that C.P.R. always works. It doesn't. However, in an emotionally charged situation many of us are reluctant to throw in the towel and "allow" the patient to die, not least because we fear accusations that we may have been negligent.

It is in an attempt to overcome the problem of lack of information before cardiac or respiratory arrest that Do Not Attempt Resuscitation (D.N.A.R.) protocols have been developed and are being used in hospitals and nursing homes in Britain. These are *not* a cost-cutting exercise, intended to increase the throughput of patients. "The decision not to resuscitate someone should be based on the concept of the right to die with dignity and without heroic (over-zealous) medical intervention."[3] While some clinicians were concerned that talking about end-of-life issues with patients might be distressing for the patients (as well as for the doctors themselves), others, especially in the areas of terminal care, could demonstrate the benefits of openness to all involved.

2 *I am indebted to Dr Anthony Handley and his article in Care of the Critically Ill, Vol.6, No.4.*

3 *Guidelines for issuing Do-not-resuscitate order at Addenbrooke's Hospital, Dr Gilbert Park, 9/3/93.*

To have engaged in discussion with the patient when this is possible and appropriate as to what he/she would wish by way of clinical intervention if the heart or breathing were to stop spontaneously raises the status of the patient from "The chronic obstructive airways disease in Bed 12" to "Mrs Jones who seems to have set her affairs in order and asks only that we keep her free of pain, ensuring that her last days are dignified."

There were those who, whether through ignorance, confusion, or prejudice, perceived the introduction of a D.N.A.R. protocol in the hospital as if it were the practice of euthanasia and expressed disapproval. On the other hand local unsolicited comments were, without exception, of welcome. I think I detected in some of them relief that the medical profession could now acknowledge that it was no longer God!

One Sunday morning I had arranged to share the bread and wine of the Holy Communion with one particularly frail patient. She had previously discussed with me her view that, when her time came, she did not want any attempt at resuscitation. That Sunday a student who was training for ordination was assigned to me. The patient, Betty, made the student welcome and we sat, one at each side of her bed. Betty joined in the brief prayers, received Communion, and laid back on her pillows. After a few moments of total stillness the student looked anxiously across the bed at me. "I think she's died," I whispered. "Would you like to go and let Staff Nurse know, or would you rather sit and hold Betty's hand while I go?" Some ten minutes later the student and I left the ward and returned to my office. It was the first time she had seen someone die and she was having difficulty taking in what a gentle and undramatic event it had been.

"When your time comes," she asked me, "what do you hope will happen to you?"

"I hope that, for so long as I need it, there'll be a human hand for me to hold. When I pass beyond the reach of that I hope there may be another hand outstretched to steady and welcome me. And I shall be enormously honoured if I find in that hand the imprint of a nail."

Years before hospitals introduced D.N.A.R. protocols Margaret was nearing the end of her life. Her rapid flow of conversation on every subject on earth prevented any discussion of the one she was trying to avoid—her own death. When she had been moved into a side room she was on her own a lot. One day she challenged me, almost aggressively, to tell her what I thought happened when we die. She did not seem convinced by what was inevitably an unsuccessful attempt by one human being to tell another human being about something neither of us had experienced. Her doubt remained and my heart felt heavier each day I visited her.

One morning the ward sister said that Margaret was weaker. I went to the side room and found her very pale and asleep. She did not appear to be breathing and, when I held her wrist, I could find no pulse. I called the ward sister and she notified the doctor. The interval before his arrival I spent in silence beside the bed wishing Margaret farewell. A couple of hours later I was called back to the ward, and I assumed that it was in order to provide support to Margaret's grieving family. The ward sister looked somewhat sheepish. "Can you go down to Side Room B? Margaret is asking for you."

She recognised me as soon as I entered her room. "Thank you for coming," she said. "I've not been well."
I smiled at her understatement and asked her how she felt now.

"Oh, I'm not too bad but I'm rather puzzled over what's been happening. I saw you come in earlier. I saw you holding my hand and praying beside my bed. I saw Sister fetching Dr N. from Ward C, but I can't understand how I could see myself as I lay unconscious in the bed and you kneeling beside it."

Never before, either in that side room or elsewhere in the hospital had I knelt beside a patient's bed. Throughout my silent prayerful vigil I had been looking at her face and closed eyes. Neither Sister nor I had been able to detect breathing or pulse. When I subsequently caught up with the doctor, a locum, I enquired whether he had, on arrival at Margaret, mentioned his name or where he had come from to resuscitate her. He admitted to being far too out of breath for such niceties. Yet he confirmed what Margaret had "seen." I invited Margaret to tell me what she thought might have been going on.

"I think I really had a glimpse of death."

"I think you might be right," I replied. "If so, how do you feel about it?"

"It was strange but wonderful. I was here and yet I could see Sister going to fetch Dr N. All the pain had gone and there was such peace. I knew what you were praying and I wanted to thank you for seeing me on my way. It was as if I was somewhere above the door, looking back down on my body in the bed. I was aware of people around me. I didn't recognise them but they were so kind. Then Doctor fiddled around with my body and — Oh, the pain!"

"If that was dying" I said as Margaret recovered her breath, "is it all that dreadful?"

"No," she said. "I'm quite looking forward to it now."

Two days later she finally lost consciousness and died peacefully.

There is a growing interest in reports of out-of-body and near-death experiences. What I find particularly noteworthy about Margaret's is that we were able to corroborate some of the detail—my kneeling beside her bed, the name of the doctor whom she had never met before, and where he was called from to resuscitate her—detail she could not have gleaned from her usual five senses. Since she was accurate in her description of so much of her experience I have to allow that she might also have been accurate about what she described of herself and of those around her as she looked back down at her body in the bed.

Except in three specific circumstances emergency ambulance crews are not allowed to declare that people are dead. In all other cases this has to be done by a doctor, even though the paramedics may be quite certain that the patient has died. For years this left ambulance crews in a cleft stick. They were certain that further attempts at C.P.R. were a waste of time, but were having to "keep going" until either a doctor arrived at the scene or until they could transfer the patient to hospital where a doctor could pronounce that life was extinct. Our local Ambulance Trust set up a pilot study in one ambulance station. The Trust's clinical director invited me to join him in a training session one evening as he briefed the crews. In cases of cardiac or respiratory arrest they were expected to go through the protocol of attempting resuscitation. What was new was this: Once they had been through that protocol and had clear evidence (in the form of the "strip"—the paper graph produced by the electrocardiograph) that cardiac function had ceased irreversibly, they were permitted to stop. They were not declaring the patient dead, but rather were given permission by the Trust to desist from a clinical activity that was ineffective and no longer appropriate. The crews asked me how they could convey this to bystanders or relatives.

I suggested that they try something like "I'm getting the feeling that this is becoming undignified." The response was likely to reveal how others perceived their efforts.

"Please don't give up—she's all I've got" suggests that the relative is not yet ready to let her go, and this may be an indication for transferring by ambulance to Accident and Emergency (A. & E.).

"Could we get him off the floor and lay him on his bed before the children arrive?" suggests a desire for dignity rather than for fruitless heroics.

I explained that I foresaw two circumstances when, in spite of fulfilling all the criteria for stopping their C.P.R., the paramedics might choose to continue and transfer the patient to hospital. The first was when the victim or crew were in danger, either from, say a collapsing building or explosion, or from hostile bystanders. They all agreed that, in such circumstances, they would "scoop and run." What, they asked, was the second circumstance?

"When it's someone you know."

There was a palpable silence while they absorbed the implications. But they agreed.

Exactly one week later, to the hour, the loudspeakers in the ambulance station announced that a paramedic ambulance crew was needed urgently at a collapse in a house. The first crew on standby were already heading for their vehicle when the address was given. It was that of the parents of the paramedic. The second crew, recognising the address, scrambled to their feet, raced into the ambulance bay and told the first crew that they would attend. "You get over to A.& E. and we'll see you there."

The first I knew of this was a little over an hour later. By chance I had decided to look in on A.& E. before heading for home, it being about 9pm.

The ambulance paramedic's mother had collapsed and now he, his wife, and father stood beside the trolley bearing her body in the resuscitation room. Also present were the full resuscitation team and a television crew. The latter were in the A.& E. Department making a documentary and had been given permission both by the family and by the hospital to be there. The camera had been recording a nurse using a telephone to put out a bleep call for me. She put down the handset and the camera panned to the door just as I walked in. The consultant, standing at the head of the trolley, called out "Bloody Radar! You've done it again!" Only then did my bleep go off with the message to ring "Resus."

I recognised the ambulance paramedic at once, but it took me a moment to register that his uniform disguised his prime role — that of a grieving relative.

I felt that the situation was too profound for words and so I stood quietly with them as they took stock of the fact that Mother had died. The next day her son, the ambulance paramedic, told me "It wasn't what you said. It was what you didn't say. Your silence spoke volumes."

The presence of the family in the resuscitation room while C.P.R. was being performed was not a special concession because the son of the patient was a member of the

Ambulance Service. It has become normal to extend an invitation to relatives to be present so long as there is a spare member of staff familiar with the procedures who is not needed to assist in the resuscitation. This "chaperone" is assigned to the family to answer their questions, escort them to the relatives' room if they choose not to stay, and to be their companion in this traumatic experience.

I was present as chaperone on the first occasion we "allowed" relatives to witness a resuscitation attempt. The parents of a teenager asked if they could sit with him during the procedure. The consultant in charge made an inspired decision to agree to their request and I put chairs for them, one on each side of the trolley. "Bagging" (pushing air into the lungs) was carried out from above the head of the trolley. Chest compressions were done from the side, and the boy's parents sat level with his knees, holding his hands. Like this they were not interfering with the attempt to re-start his heart but were doing what only they could do— "being there" for him. They saw the physical exertion and beads of sweat on the forehead of the staff nurse doing the chest compression. They recognised and commented that the only time the heart monitor trace showed any movement was during those compressions. And they were reminded to let go of his hands while the defibrillator sent an electrical impulse through his chest to try to "kick-start" his heart. They saw the effort being put into trying to save their son's life, and it was they who indicated when they felt it was time to stop.

The consultant looked at each member of the resuscitation team and everyone nodded agreement. What happened next was so simple and yet so profound. Without any fuss the airway was disconnected, the cardiac monitor was turned off, and all the resuscitation team quietly left the room. The only people who did not move were the lad and his parents. I looked to them for guidance and when they said they were all right I said that I would wait just outside the door.

For years I had been involved in the alternative scenario. The family are ushered into a room, often without windows. They can hear the wail of bleeps, the running feet, and their imaginations run riot. They have seen "Casualty", "E.R.", and countless other hospital documentaries, and they roll all these fantasies into one—one going on only a few feet from them. After an age the door opens and a doctor and nurse enter. If I have been sitting with the relatives I can feel the spasm of tension in them as they brace themselves for the news. When they are up to accepting the invitation to go through to the resuscitation room to be with "the deceased" they approach a doorway into a room in which (say) Father fought his last and greatest battle—for life itself—and lost. Some people's knees give way as they cross the threshold. Others turn and run screaming out of the building. But all of them acknowledge one thing. They were not with him when he died. However hard we try to ease this self-reproach with "But he knew nothing after he collapsed at home," they are frequently haunted by the feeling that they had let him down and had deserted him when he needed them most. Instead he had died among strangers.

After the death of the teenage boy we began to question whether relatives were more traumatised by being present during an unsuccessful resuscitation attempt than by being excluded. The Texas Revised Inventory of Grief was used in an attempt to make an objective assessment of which relatives fared better—those who accepted the invitation to be present or those who either declined the invitation or were not asked.[4]   In the early stages of what became a research study, in an effort to provide a valid basis for comparison, some relatives were invited to be present, and others were not.

A statistically approved method of randomising the invitation was used. However, as the study progressed the staff taking part said that they felt it was so right that they invite the relatives to be present that we scrapped the randomising. The families who had chosen to be present were consistently scoring so much better — indicating a more positive adjustment to their loss — that it was considered unethical to exclude anyone from the invitation to be present.

So far as I can remember, by the time the project was complete there had been only two complaints. Both were from people who had declined the invitation to be present. They felt that we should have tried harder to persuade them to sit with their relatives during the resuscitation attempts!

There are doctors and nurses who cannot accept the results of the research. It is up to them to defend themselves against the charge of prejudice and of placing their own

---

4   *The Texas Revised Inventory of Grief, developed in the late 1970s by Dr Thomas Faschingbauer and others, was the first coherent test for measuring and comparing people's grief reactions to bereavement. The questionnaire was in two parts. The first invited respondents to think back to the time of bereavement (e.g."8. I often dreamed about the person"). The second part enquired of present feelings (e.g. "46. I still get angry when I think of him/her"). Respondents would tick how true or false each statement was for them. The researcher would use a transparent scoring template, placed over the answered questionnaire, to convert the ticks into a numerical score — low for a low level of grief, and high for a high level. A high score for the first part followed by a low score in the second was interpreted as an acute grief which had been resolved.*

comfort and convenience above the proven benefits to their patients' families.

In an article in *The Observer* ("The real E.R." 7/12/97) the Editor of *The Lancet*, Dr Richard Horton described how, as a junior doctor, he had had to tell a woman, waiting with her daughters, that her husband had died. "It was, needless to say, all wrong." He concluded that our research project "had overturned the groundless dogma that excludes relatives from the scene of a resuscitation. All relatives entering Addenbrooke's at similar times of crisis are now offered the chance to be present in the resuscitation room. Not everyone takes up the offer. But I wish I had had the opportunity to invite that family to join their husband and father to say goodbye. Properly."[5]

---

5 *Copyright Guardian Newspapers Limited 1997.*

The paranormal

It was three o'clock on a March morning when I was called in to an Acute Medical ward. The staff had a hunch that the 29-year-old son of a dying man could do with someone to share his bedside vigil. It was necessary to tread carefully to avoid encroaching on his privacy. I approached the bed carrying two mugs. "The staff asked me to bring you a coffee. May I join you with mine?"

His need for refreshment overcame his resistance to the intrusion of this stranger, and I was invited to sit on the chair on the opposite side of the bed to him so long as I promised not to talk about religion. His father's breathing was typical of someone near the end of life. A short intake of breath was followed immediately by a sigh as the patient exhaled. There was then a pause of eight or ten seconds before the next breath. Each pause could have extended for ever. The young man began to talk about his father—how devoted his parents had been to each other, and how heartbroken his father had been when his mother died seven years earlier. The son had found it hard to keep his father motivated to feed and care for himself, and now he had suffered a stroke which had resulted in his admission to hospital.

As we spoke I noticed that his father's breathing had changed. It now had a normal rhythm, like ours. Having been profoundly unconscious he opened his eyes, sat up, and reached out both arms to the foot of his bed with a broad smile of recognition. I am told that when the part of the brain controlling movement is damaged the arms can move in a particular way. This "extension" results in the palms of the hands facing away from each other when the arms are straight out. That was not the case here. What the son and I saw was typical of someone reaching out in welcome. We both looked to the foot of the bed, following the patient's ecstatic gaze. I did not see anything, but I felt a warmth on my cheek, such as would have been caused by a light or a fire at the foot of the bed. The son called out "Mother!" When we looked back at his father we saw that he had lain back on his pillows, his eyes closed, his hands by his side, and his life over.

I have no idea how long we sat stunned and silent. When one person experiences the presence of a loved one who has died it is often presumed to be wishful thinking. When two people share the same event it is less easy to dismiss it as auto-suggestion. But when three people are simultaneously affected by the same experience it is much more difficult to explain away. The staff confirmed that the patient had died. The son and I sat in the ward office while his father's belongings were assembled and handed over in the inevitable plastic bag. We left the building and walked out to the hospital car park six floors below as dawn was breaking. The air was still and the dawn chorus of birdsong was the only sound. He leant on his car door and looked back up at the window next to which lay his dead father. He said "No one could ever have told me that I would be leaving here so convinced of what happened on the first Easter Day."

Peter was 14 and desperately ill. He had lost his ability to resist infection and was not likely to survive. Indeed, both the consultant in charge and I had left messages with the ward staff that if he deteriorated we were to be called. The word "deteriorated" was something of a euphemism since Peter was only just hanging on to life.

I looked in on him one morning, surprised that I had not been called during the night. His mother had stayed with him and now, although tired, was keen to see me. "Peter's got something he wants to tell you," she said.

I glanced at Peter, lying exhausted in the bed, and suggested that I call in again so that he could tell me when he was feeling a bit stronger. This resulted in the slightest hint of a nod from the pillow. The next day the staff told me that there were signs that Peter was beginning to overcome the infection. I tiptoed into his room. Both he and his mother were awake.

"You know I wasn't well the night before last."

"Yes," I replied hesitantly, wondering both at the understatement and where this conversation was going.

"I had a visitor."

"Really," I said. "Who was it?"

"I don't know. I couldn't see him, but I know he was here."

"How did you know he was here?"

"I was trying to use the bottle in the bed, but it was in the wrong place and I didn't want to have an accident. My hands were too swollen and sore to hold it. But he moved it for me so that it didn't spill."

His mother cut in with "I saw that bottle move entirely on its own."

"How did you feel about this visitor you couldn't see—happy, sad, hot, cold, frightened, spooky, or how?"

"Oh no! He was a friend. And he came again last night." As an afterthought he added "I didn't think I believed in angels."

"You lucky devil!" I replied. "All of us grown-ups who have spent a lifetime longing for evidence that we are surrounded by God and all his helpers, and you, you jammy dodger — you've been given that evidence at the age of 14."

I think he had been afraid that I might have ridiculed his interpretation of what happened. In the event his parents and grandparents told me they were grateful that I had affirmed his experience rather than dismissing it as feverish delirium. He astounded us all by making a complete recovery and, when I was in touch with him years later, he remembered the incident clearly.

It must have been a couple of years after Peter's stay on the ward that a Roman Catholic priest had arranged to spend a day "shadowing" me within the hospital. We had been visiting an adult patient in the single room which Peter had occupied. I do not recall anything noteworthy about our visit, but my colleague said as we left the ward "The air in that room was crackling with the Holy Spirit!"

I told him about Peter's experience.

"Wow!" he exclaimed. "We have been entertaining angels unawares!"

In my experience early morning sunlight in April has a particular clarity and brilliance. I have no idea whether it is because showers have cleared the atmosphere of dust particles or because, after the overcast months of winter, I had forgotten how clear the sunlight can be. It was at 5.30 one such April morning that I was on a ward where a woman was dying. The staff had called me because they were puzzled by her claim that she could see someone, in addition to her husband, in the room. Hallucination can be caused by some medicines, and by low blood oxygen, but there was a coherence in her perception which made either of these explanations less likely. I was taken by the staff nurse into the single room where she lay.

"He's here!" she called out excitedly.

Staff Nurse replied "Yes. This is Ian, our chaplain. I promised you he would come."

"No! No!" said the patient, and to me "Can't you see him?"

"Tell me," I said. "What does he look like?" I was only aware of the brilliantly sunlit room in which we were.

"Oh! look at him. I know it's him. Look at the marks in his hands, and feet, and side, and, Oh!, what a lovely smile!"

"Is that all right?" I asked.

"It's more than all right. It's wonderful!" she replied.

I was aware that the room had been brilliantly lit by the early morning sun, but that now it was less bright, possibly because of some passing cloud.

"He's gone now" said the patient.

Her husband, sitting beside her asked if she had seen a vision.

"No!" was her reply. "That wasn't a vision. That was real. He's ready for me now."

"Who the hell's she talking about?" demanded her husband, a pigeon-fancier.

I explained that I could only think of one person with wounds in hands, feet, and side. It was clear from his reaction that neither he nor his wife were familiar with the Gospel accounts of Jesus' appearances after his crucifixion.

He seemed to find it best to dismiss his wife's experience as fantasy. She, however, was perceptibly more relaxed and spent the last hour and a half of her life asleep. After we had left the room Staff Nurse thanked me for my input in the case. I said that I thought there had been an input far more significant than mine!

Just as Christmas Eve is the day before Christmas, so Hallowe'en is the day before the Feast of All Hallows, otherwise known as All Saints' Day. It was during the afternoon of Hallowe'en, October 31st, that the charge nurse on an Acute Psychiatric ward asked me to look in so as to discuss the care of one of the patients. The young man in question had been admitted suffering from acute depression. He had, I was assured, not previously shown any symptoms of paranoid delusions, yet he was insisting that he must leave hospital that evening in order to attend the witches' coven of which he was a member. This was way outside the experience of the nursing staff—hence the call to me, not that I was all that familiar with such proceedings.

I invited the young man to describe how the evening "meeting" was likely to involve him. From his description I suspected that his attendance would be more of a duty than pleasure. He insisted that, if he was not at the coven, then the others would come and get him, in spite of their being some twenty-five miles away in his home village. This gave me the chance to ask him directly "Do you really want to go through all this pelting rain to be with them this evening? Or would you rather stay with us in the warm and dry? If you are frightened that the other members of the coven might come and try to get you we can make sure that the ward is secure. If you like I could come and be here at midnight for a while so that, if they try to get you, they'll have to get me first."

Whether it was the foul weather or my offer to do a "stakeout" he decided not to discharge himself. With his permission I made a telephone call to his local vicar, to whom he was known. I outlined the story we had been told and was taken aback by his matter-of-fact response that the villagers were fed up with discovering decapitated cockerels and blood spattered on gravestones in the churchyard. The local police were apparently following up the complaints as a public nuisance enquiry. The vicar thought that the staff's and my approach, being low-key but affirmative, was probably wise, and he wished us well.

I turned up, as agreed, soon after 11pm on the ward. Most of the patients were in bed or on the way there. The young man who had decided not to be the 13th member of the coven was sitting with the night staff, and I joined them. From midnight he was very agitated, but we did our best to reassure him. At 12.40 he suddenly relaxed. The change in him was dramatic. "They're not going to get me now. I think I'll head for bed."

The male nurse in charge offered to accompany him upstairs but he was feeling sufficiently self-confident not to need an escort. By 1.00am he was asleep, and so I decided that I could reasonably end my vigil and head home to my own bed. The staff promised to bleep me if they were concerned.

During the night the rain stopped, the sky cleared, and All Saints' Day dawned with a beautiful hoar frost. I cycled across to the ward and was greeted by the day staff who could not believe the change in our young patient. He was relaxed, communicative, far less withdrawn—indeed quite expansive. It seemed as if he had, with our help, broken the controlling stricture of a group who had been dominating him. Later in the morning I had a telephone call from the young man's vicar, enquiring how things had gone at our end. I explained how he had been very twitched from midnight, but that shortly before 1am he had concluded that he was safe and had gone to bed.

"That's interesting," said the vicar. "The police rumbled the coven at twenty to one."

Words and silence

What can you say to someone who has been bereaved? This
question, posed to seminars of senior nurses and midwives,
produced some interesting responses. They were very clear
about what you should *not* say. One supervisor of midwives
described as "pukeworthy" the statement at the head of a
commercially produced handout provided by her hospital
for bereaved families: "May I, on behalf of S. Swithin's
Hospital NHS Trust, convey to you our condolences at your
sad loss." Other similarly vacuous, crass, insincere, or even
downright cruel comments were reported. I invited the
participants each to write down one such statement. I then
placed a waste paper bin in the middle of the circle in which
we were all sitting. One by one they read out the platitude
they had written down, screwed up the piece of paper, and,
promising never to say what was written on it, threw it into
the bin. There were laughs and groans in equal measure as
the list grew:

"It had to be."   "No it didn't. It was only because you
cocked up his care that he died."

"She's had a good innings." "Maybe, but she still had some
more runs to score."

"Time's a wonderful healer. You'll get over it." "How dare
you talk of my life's partner as 'it'. I'm not sure I ever want
to 'get over' losing her."

"You're still young. You can try for another baby." "This
baby carried all our hopes and love. Don't write him off as
replaceable."

We concluded that, in general, saying something — anything
— made the person making the comment feel better, but did
nothing for the bereaved. If that is so then are we not
abusing them for our own ends?

We are told that, alone in the animal kingdom, humans use speech to communicate, and we presuppose that it is the highest form of communication. That does not mean that it is the most profound. With some insight participants in the seminars would offer the view that, in the most intense of human experiences, words were an intrusion. One of the best comments was reported as having been made by a neighbour of someone recently bereaved. Apparently he stood awkwardly on the doorstep and said diffidently "I didn't know what to say, so I've come to say it." Other comments reported were of the type "He's gone to a better place." Staff were cautious about criticising such statements but many were clearly uneasy about them. We agreed that this was no time to challenge the beliefs, either of those making these comments or of the bereaved themselves. Yet there were grounds for concern. Whether or not their belief could be substantiated, was it going to help them adjust effectively to the loss of the physical presence and companionship of, say, their life's partner? Whenever he or she had gone away previously he had returned. The language of "gone to a better place" carries with it the luggage of past experience "but will be coming home next week/month." Even the terminology of the well-used passage ascribed variously to Victor Hugo and Bishop C.H. Brent can be construed as long-term removal or emigration.[6]

Seminar participants were often surprised to find that there was no research evidence to support the notion that those

6 *"A ship sails and I stand watching till she fades on the horizon and someone at my side says, 'She is gone.' Gone where? Gone from my sight, that is all; she is just as large as when I saw her. The diminished size and total loss of sight is in me, not in her, and just at the moment when someone at my side says 'She is gone,' there are others who are watching her coming, and other voices take up a glad shout, 'There she comes!' And that is dying."*

with a religious belief find bereavement less traumatic than those who have no such belief.

We cited examples from our own experience of recently bereaved people who had laid a place at the dining table for the person who had died, as if forgetting that he would not be needing it; of others who had become so used to visiting at the hospital or hospice that they would turn up at visiting time even after the patient had died. These and other instances were described not with condemnation but with compassion for the anguish suffered by the bereaved when they realised their mistakes. My own inclination when listening to recently bereaved people is not to initiate comments of the type "He'll be happy in Heaven," but to note when they volunteer such an opinion. Only then do I probe gently as to whether this helps them with their loss. Occasionally my enquiry is perceived as giving them permission for an outburst such as "How can I be content that he/she is happy anywhere other than with me?" It seems as if such people imagine that clergy and ministers require that they say something "religious", when deep down they want to rant and rage at the God they claim they don't believe in. I would much rather face this onslaught of passionate honesty than waste their and my time in dishonest platitudes. After all, we are both confronted with a reality which cannot be revoked — a death. Some people may engage in denial as a mechanism for handling the enormity of this reality, but I do not see it as my role to use my belief in Heaven to reinforce their denial of the fact of death.

One man apologised to me for the expletives he was using against God. He admitted surprise that I had smiled rather than been offended. He asked why.

"For you to get so angry with God is perfectly understandable when your wife has just died. Yours is the impotent fury of someone who would have given everything to keep her alive and well. In that there's no-one bigger upon whom you can vent your fury you're taking it out on God. You don't get angry with someone who means nothing to you. You don't waste time or energy on them. By getting so angry with Him you have probably taken Him more seriously than you've ever done before. After all, if He's worthy of the name God He's big enough to take a bit of stick from His friends!"

As an example I cited my hazy recollection of a story about St Teresa of Avila. Apparently she was travelling in an ox cart when the axle broke, tipping her out of the cart into a ditch. As she sat up to her waist in muddy water she shook her fist, exclaiming "God! If this is the lousy way you treat your friends it's no wonder you have so few!"

One of the most bizarre instances of the denial of the reality of a death I have come across was when two sisters took their elderly father in a wheelchair window shopping and to the local park for weeks after he had died. Only when the neighbours complained of the smell from their house did environmental health officers discover his decomposing body in his armchair. Even then his daughters insisted that he must not be removed until he had finished watching *Coronation Street*.

In other seminars, with theological students, I would use different terminology. When, later in their lives, they are visiting the newly bereaved they may be tempted to presuppose that, because such people have been churchgoers, they will be convinced that, say, Grandad is in

Heaven. My concern is that they avoid putting Grandma into "doctrinal short circuit". In the first weeks and months following his death she is trying to adjust to his absence after what might have been sixty years together. To require her to come to terms with his permanent absence from her and in the next breath to delight in his partying in Heaven may result in such a demand of emotional and intellectual energy that she is overloaded and "blows a fuse". I have lost count of the number of clinical and nursing staff who have asked me to visit such patients. Typically they are bewildered that their "faith has deserted them", that they had previously thought that "God was their friend". Their presupposition had been that belief in God would protect them from bereavement and its consequent anguish—both invalid and previously untested. Now they are bewildered and depressed that life itself is intolerable, and they, too, want to die. Up until now the study of their scriptures, attendance at church, chapel, meeting house, mosque, synagogue, or temple once or more a week has met their religious, spiritual, and social needs. Few of them have tested the myth and metaphor of their religious language against the uncompromising reality of physical death. Trying to make the connection so blew the minds of some theological students that they gave up. Is it any wonder that other people, with less theological, philosophical, and psychological equipment, *and* at a time of enormous emotional trauma, "blow a fuse"?

A young woman lay injured in hospital. Her two little children were dead. I sat silently beside her bed, uncertain as to whether I was acceptable. Her first words to me were "What makes you think there's a God?" None of the conventional historical arguments for the existence of God which I had learnt in order to pass exams seemed remotely relevant to her predicament.

A couple of weeks later, as she began the long process of recovery, we were walking in the hospital grounds. "They were lovely kids," she said.

"I know," I replied.

"Have you seen photographs of them?"

"Yes, but I have also seen them."

"When?"

"The day after they died. I took your family to the chapel of rest to identify them and to say goodbye. They were indeed lovely children."

She stopped and turned to face me. "You really do believe in God, don't you?"

Puzzled by this sudden twist in the conversation I replied that I do, but then enquired what made her ask.

"The night after they died, when you first came to see me, I asked you what made you think there's a God. You didn't give me the answer I expected. You said that you had been given so much evidence, all of it undeserved, that there is a God, that you don't have the luxury of being able to doubt it. I didn't expect you to say that."

Had I spoken of her little ones being safe and happy in Heaven I think I would have reinforced the sense of Hell in which she felt she was.

One Friday morning I was sitting beside the bed of an unconscious baby. Her mother, a practising Roman Catholic, sat holding her limp hand. The ventilator was doing her breathing, otherwise there was no movement.

There are those who tell me I should be using such times to remind the mother of God's infinite mercy, of Christ's blood shed for the forgiveness of her and her daughter's sins. My own instinct was to stay there, silently sharing the anguish and helplessness. Only after the mother said "I'm this child's mother and I can't do a thing to help" did I feel permitted to speak.

"That puts you in a pretty close position to Our Lady this Good Friday morning."[7]

Throughout the usual celebrations of Easter Day in that and other hospitals I had in my mind's eye the experience that family was undergoing. While others rehearsed the story of Christ's rising from the grave, they were preparing to take leave of their baby, and to lay her in a grave. Talk of resurrection and Heaven would have fallen on deaf ears that Easter Day. She died on Easter Monday morning.

Subsequently the family asked if they could provide the hospital with the one thing they felt it lacked—a chapel. Their vigil would have been more bearable had there been a place of prayer, of sanctuary, to which they could resort in order to lick their spiritual wounds and to regain strength. The enthusiasm among the staff, of all disciplines, was astonishing. A site, just off the main corridor, was identified. While friends in the family's home town raised funds, working parties on site prepared the foundations.

I shall long remember the sight of surgeons, anaesthetists, medical physics technicians, and others, wielding picks and shovels. A builder of my acquaintance volunteered to build the duct for the electricity, water, and heating, charging only for the materials. Then his own daughter became unwell. She was treated in the hospital, and made a full recovery.

7 *The Gospel of John, chapter 19, records that Mary, the mother of Jesus, was standing near his cross as he was dying.*

Her father was so overwhelmed with thankfulness that he insisted on donating the materials as well. The "portachapel'"arrived on the back of a lorry and was lowered on to its footings. A local TV reporter enquired if it had a spire (it didn't).

I planned decoration and furnishings to enhance the sense of warmth, comfort, and safety as a contrast to the harsh lights of the wards and intensive care unit. To this end I called in at a carpet shop I passed frequently. I explained to the owner the effect I wanted to achieve and the floor area I needed covered. He enquired what sort of room and what was its function. Only then did I explain that this was for the new hospital chapel. Suddenly he sat down heavily on a pile of carpets. "You'll never believe this. My wife had open heart surgery at the hospital yesterday. I'll beat any quotation you get!"

The gathering to celebrate the opening of the new chapel included the family of the baby who had died at Easter the previous year, augmented by her two-week-old sister. Seven weeks later the local Anglican bishop was sitting in the chapel with me. "People tell me," he said "that medieval churches have a special atmosphere because centuries of prayer have been absorbed by the stonework. This place has only existed for a couple of months, and yet it has just as strong an atmosphere about it."

The night porters told me that when they were carrying out their security rounds of the hospital they would often sneak into the chapel and sit for a few minutes. They always felt safe and welcome.

Fever hospitals and tuberculosis sanatoria used to be built outside smoky cities so that patients could breathe clean air. Leeds had expanded to surround one such hospital which stood on a hill overlooking the city. In the late 1970s and 1980s there were hardly any cases of T.B., but there were other respiratory diseases, among them lung cancer, requiring treatment. One man tried to enlist my help in getting a cigarette to fit through a hole in his oxygen mask! The nursing staff, whom I alerted, did not think he was suicidal, but we agreed that, had he succeeded in lighting up, he would have been killed by the resulting conflagration.

Elsewhere in that hospital, in a single room, lay a woman in her early sixties. On her bedside locker was a photograph of her, taken a couple of years earlier, at the helm of the small yacht which she and her husband had enjoyed sailing. Now she was hardly conscious. Her husband told me that she had been a great churchgoer and believed in "Heaven and all that". He had not been against that kind of thing, indeed he wished she was still conscious so that, among other things, she could help him through his doubts.

"I suppose you've come to tell me I've got to trust in God."

"No," was my reply. "If I've come to tell you anything it is to let you know that I trust in Him, and that if you want to lean on me for a while you are welcome to do so."

This roused his curiosity and we were soon engrossed in conversation beside his wife's bed.

"I am convinced that there is a God, and that He is already taking care of your wife. You are not sure. You fear there may be nothing after this life and that you'll never see her again. Yet you tell me that you would like to believe in Heaven and in a joyful reunion there. If there is no heaven, and if there is no god, then as the hormones, enzymes, and proteins bring my body to a final grinding halt, I shall know nothing. I shall have that absence of consciousness which makes sleep so welcome—no dreams, no bleep calls to wake me up—nothing, neither the knowledge of being wrong nor the regret that I shan't see any of my loved ones again. If, on the other hand, there is life beyond the grave then everything I've worked and prayed for will be fulfilled. And when we meet I promise not to gloat!"

Capitalising on his nautical experience I offered a simile. "Tonight you are like someone who is convinced that the world is flat. If you go beyond Wakefield you'll fall off the edge. I am convinced that the world is round, and that it is safe beyond Wakefield for you, for your wife, and for me. I can't convince you it is round. I can only offer you my hand as we find ourselves approaching what you fear is the edge over which your wife is about to fall. I am ready to risk what you think is that fall so that you needn't be alone."

Late that night after his wife had died he and I walked out to the hospital car park. We stopped beside his car and he looked out over the city. In the distance the sodium lights illuminated the route of the M 1 on its way south. With one hand he took my arm, and with the other he pointed to the horizon, saying "It is all right beyond Wakefield!"

My confidence that there is life beyond death (and Wakefield) led to my being challenged in a discussion on local radio. Mixed church groups had been meeting to address aspects of the Christian faith and were encouraged to telephone the radio station with questions. I had been asked to join the local Roman Catholic bishop in the studio to field the calls. One was directed specifically at me.

Margaret, the person deputed to pose the question over the telephone knew me already, and I recognised her voice.

"If Heaven is where God is, and God is everywhere, how can there be another place called Hell?"

We had been given no notice of the questions and so it was necessary to think fast.

"Let us imagine that you have been a lifelong supporter of Leeds United. You have paid your subscription and in fair weather and foul you have stood on the terraces at Elland Road watching your team being trounced. Today — miracle of miracles! — United is actually winning at home!"

The producer of the radio programme jumped up and down exclaiming "You'll have us sued out of existence!" The laughter over the telephone line from Margaret and the rest of her house group was broadcast all over West Yorkshire.

"You are in your seventh heaven. This is the fulfilment of all you have ever hoped for. I am standing right next to you — same time, same place, same experience. However, I don't understand the first thing about football. The happier you are, the more lost and alienated and cold and wet I feel. I am in sheer hell. Now the main difference between the image of the football match and Heaven is that the one lasts 90 minutes with oranges and a band at half time, and the other goes on for ever. To be eternally confronted with the ideals of love, gentleness, and forgiveness when, by an act of your own will, you choose to be at odds with such ideals — that strikes me as a fair definition of Hell, especially since you can't escape from it."

A prayer which, for centuries, has been used within the Christian Church at the time of death and at funerals includes variations on the theme: "Go on your journey, dear

Christian soul, ... May the angels of God watch around you and protect you, ...The saints of God pray for you, ... May your rest today be in peace and your home in the paradise of God."

The parents of a baby and I stood together at his graveside. As I began the prayer I thought that its language was a bit heavy for them and so, on the spur of the moment, I changed it. "May the angels of God watch around you and protect you, the saints of God welcome you and play with you..."

As we left the grave and walked back to their car the mother said "Only this morning our nine-year-old daughter asked if there would be anyone in Heaven to play with Michael."

On other occasions external factors provided the inspiration for images of Heaven. Toby was in his forties when he had a heart attack and died. He had spent years in an institution for adults with learning difficulties. He had no relatives. We, the staff, and his fellow residents were his family. At the crematorium there were a dozen of us—staff and residents—to see him off. Simple, direct, truthful, and affectionate language was required. Just as the curtains were closing around Toby's coffin my bleep went off. For a moment I tried to cover my confusion and then I had a thought. Toby loved *Star Trek*. It was his favourite television programme. He called Kirk "Noddy" and Spock "Big Ears". And so I pulled my bleep out of my pocket and, holding it as the characters in *Star Trek* did, I said "Right, Lord, you can beam him up now!" Most of those within the crematorium chapel took the point and laughed.

This clearly unscripted insertion seemed to respect the unique importance of the occasion and to emphasise what I was trying to say about Toby being safely back on board the eternal star ship Enterprise.

The crematorium staff conceded afterwards that they liked the genuineness of funerals from the hospital. The residents and staff attended because they wanted to, rather than out of any sense of duty or because they hoped for a share in the dead person's estate.

A young couple serving with the U.S. Air Force in England had a stillborn baby. They asked me to arrange for him to be buried in a country churchyard near their base. Many churchyards are full, but because this was going to require only a tiny plot it was possible to locate it beneath a flowering cherry tree near the west end of the church. As the tall serviceman from the Deep South, wearing his black tuxedo, carried the little white coffin towards the grave he had to stoop beneath the branches. I noticed a bird perched above us. The coffin was lowered and the bird flew out of the tree. It was a white dove, and one of its feathers floated gracefully down, straight into the grave, landing on the coffin. Walt Disney could not have contrived it better. When all the mourners had left, and only the gravedigger and I remained, I reached down into the grave and retrieved the feather. Holding it up in the branches where the dove had perched I released it and we watched it float down on to the grass. Despite several such attempts I could not get it to enter the grave and land on the coffin. In the end I gave up and replaced it there.

Like the bleep in Toby's funeral, the feather in this one was effective as an image because it was unscripted and "given". I wonder to what extent Christ used simple and commonplace images of Heaven not only to catch the imagination of his hearers, but also to convey how natural and obvious a sequel to this life Heaven is.

Jack was in his 90s. His mind was as sharp as ever but his health was failing. In particular, his eyesight and ability to walk were severely limited. On the day of his funeral the flag at his Golf Club was flying at half mast. Had they had flagpoles I have no doubt that his local bookmakers would also have marked the occasion. I had known him for some time, and I gather he was thankful that I did not talk "religion". This extract of his funeral service is quoted with his daughters' permission.

"It was a week ago this evening that I was sitting with Jack. There was the customary concern that I was comfortable, that this was my busy day (he clearly thought it was Sunday) and that there must be others more deserving of my time than him. When I replied that there was no one I would rather be with than him at that moment he replied with his characteristic self-effacing but dismissive grunt. He wanted a drink of water but insisted on holding the glass on his own, allowing me to take it once he had finished. In spite of admitting to feeling so ill there was clear evidence of his independent spirit and of his gracious dignity. He felt for my hand and thanked me for visiting him.

On Sunday morning I knelt beside his bed ten minutes after he died. As I closed his eyes I thought 'Until now you've been seeing through a glass darkly. Now I pray that you can see face to face. After your recent struggle to walk unaided I hope that you can stride along the fairways of heaven.' I allowed myself a mischievous thought that perhaps even the four horses of the Apocalypse would now have been given racing colours and form! I recalled our conversations about railways and our agreement that Ely station was the draughtiest and (with fish boxes on the platform) the smelliest in East Anglia. He had laughed at my quotation of Wilbert Awdry — him of *Thomas the Tank Engine* — explaining why so many Church of England clergy were steam train fanatics. Both the Railways and the Church, Awdry explained, had their heyday in the Victorian era. Both were encumbered with large buildings which were expensive to maintain. Both were the butt of ridicule, and both were convinced that they had the best means of getting mankind to his ultimate destination. Jack, it is my prayer for you that you have arrived safely, and have been met on the platform by those who have known and loved you. I hesitate to burden you by asking any more favours of you, but it would be comforting for us to know that you might find time within eternity to be on the platform when our trains pull in."

Early one Saturday morning I was sitting with the parents of a 12-year-old who had just died. The mother was on one side of the bed, and I sat next to the father on the other side. For half an hour none of us said anything. Then the father sighed "Why? Why?"

I bit my lip to remind myself to keep quiet. Experience had taught me that asking the question is generally more important than answering it. In the circumstances I thought it was an eminently fair question to ask of each other, of me, of the doctors, even of God. The child's mother responded to her husband's question with "At the moment we ask the question but don't get an answer. One day we'll be given the answer but by then will no longer be needing to ask the question."

I looked across at her and thought "You incredible woman! This is your third child to have died of cystic fibrosis, and you can say that?"

Sometimes we are perceived to speak eloquently of Heaven even when in fact we not only feel far from competent to do so but are struggling to find speech at all. The funeral of an eleven-month-old whom I had known all her life was particularly challenging. I endorse her mother's description of her as "our witty little toughy"; beyond that, words fail me.

Another couple were referred to me by their health visitor. They had been with the British Army in Germany when their third child was born. Since he was found to have a major complication after he was born the baby was flown to England where he died in hospital. His parents and brother and sister also returned home, the Army taking care of all the funeral arrangements. Months later it appeared to the health visitor that the parents were "stuck" in their bereavement. On visiting them I discovered that they had never seen their baby after he was delivered. We managed to obtain photographs of him, taken in the hospital upon his return to England and we sat together holding these, the only tangible evidence that he had existed. Talking about him became easier, especially for the children. Over the months my visits to their house became a pleasure as I observed the family beginning to "walk tall" again. When the daughter was due to be admitted to hospital for the removal of her tonsils she asked me to be her friend and to accompany her to the operating theatre. Some months later there was excitement and apprehension in equal measure at the prospect of another baby.

It was Sunday afternoon when I was called to the operating theatre. Quite often theatres are noisy, with music, the clattering of surgical instruments, instructions, and conversations. This time there was silence. A new-born babe lay dead on the operating table. My first priority was the support of the theatre staff. It was some moments before I noted the family name — and then the terrible truth dawned on me. Elsewhere, on the delivery unit, were the parents I had been trying to help back on to their feet. This child, too, had a heart defect which was not susceptible to surgical repair.

On arrival at the delivery unit I went first to the staff office where the midwives were stunned at the tragedy. One of them took me in to the room where the couple were. On entering I don't know which of us was the most tearful. I knelt down beside the bed and hugged them both. After a while I sat back on my haunches on the floor. Softly, but with a confidence I still find devastating, the grieving mother said "I have often wondered what God's face looks like. When you came in just now I knew." She was not saying, or even implying, that I looked like God. Her perception of the face of God was of One who could relate to her anguish and support her through it.

It was when I was broken, vulnerable, and at my least eloquent that perhaps I was, just for that moment, an unobstructed conduit for God's compassion and love.

While we are busy trying to find words for profound occasions we are tainting the message with our own interpretation of that message. Words may be the highest form of communication, but in the context of bereavement my experience is that the vulnerability of companionable silence is a more profound means of communicating human and, apparently in this case, divine love.

Transplants

There is no legal definition of death. Some people find this surprising, especially when there are legal procedures following a death. In most cases a legally registered medical practitioner has to certify that death has occurred. Only certain people are competent in law to register the death. And there is a legal duty to notify the Registrar of Deaths that the burial or cremation has indeed taken place.

We think we know when someone has died. Traditionally we have relied on observation that breathing and heartbeat have ceased permanently. Logically it could be claimed that we have to wait a long time to be sure that the absence of respiration and cardiac activity are permanent and irreversible. Maybe there was some merit, generations ago, in having "Grandma"in her coffin for some days in the front parlour before the funeral. Not only could the neighbourhood call and pay their respects, but it also gave time for the family to recognise that she was not going to start breathing again.

Reports of the successful resuscitation of people presumed dead are not new. One of the earliest is allegedly recorded in the Old Testament of the bible[8], over 2,500 years ago. Modern surgical techniques have challenged the traditional view that death is defined by the cessation of heartbeat. Open heart surgery requires that the heart be stopped and its function taken over by an external heart/lung machine. Only if we want to achieve dramatic effect do we say that the patient "was dead for 40 minutes on the operating table". In reality we know that the absence of heartbeat was temporary and necessary in order to enable surgery to be carried out.

---

8   *Second Book of Kings, Chapter 4, verse 32 onwards.*

The heart/lung machine ensures that the brain and other organs continue to receive oxygenated blood even when the heart is stopped for surgical repair.

Somewhere there may be a man or woman who owes their life to my absence from the hospital. I was at the local blood transfusion centre donating plasma and white cells when my bleep went off. Because there were needles in both arms I could not move to hold the telephone handset. One of the Transfusion Service staff dialled the number and held the telephone so that I could speak to my caller. It was a surgeon who had made numerous attempts to get his patient's heart going again after surgery involving the use of a heart/lung machine. He explained that he wanted me to "happen by" so as to support the family when he had to explain to them that, in spite of his best endeavours, the patient had died. I pointed out that I was immobile, heparinised, and couldn't get to him for at least an hour.

"Damn!" he said. "I'll have to try again."

He did, and the heart started.

Among the people who have confided in me their preference for burial or cremation there is a small number who include something like this: "I don't want to be buried. I couldn't stand the idea of being shut up in a coffin, feeling it being lowered into the ground and having earth shovelled in on top of me, and then suffocating." Others insist "I'm not letting anyone cremate me. The idea that I could still be alive in my coffin when it is rolled into the cremator with the roar of flames all around me. Oh no! I'm not having that!"

A Home Office pathologist, Professor Austin Gresham, tells me that, from time to time, he receives requests from solicitors acting on behalf of people who have died.

Their clients had left instructions that, after death, an artery was to be severed so as to ensure that there was no chance of reviving once inside a coffin.

An alternative approach to the fear of being "buried alive" has been provided by Fabrizio Caselli, a watchmaker in Tuscany. The *Daily Telegraph* reported on 16 October, 1995 that Caselli is prepared to provide coffins equipped with radio beacon, microphone, loudspeaker, torch, oxygen cylinder, cardiac monitor, and defibrillator. I am assured that anyone needing the use of a defibrillator would be in no fit state to use it, since they would not be conscious. Furthermore the oxygen cylinder would have to be large to allow time for the relatives to pick up the radio alarm signal and with or without a Home Office exhumation order, get to and open up the grave of the not-departed. None of this equipment would be permitted in a coffin which was to be cremated. I have seen the damage done to a hospital incinerator by an oxygen cylinder. At a crematorium the explosion would be enormous.

Old Highgate Cemetery in London contains evidence that the Victorians were fearful of being buried alive. Some mausolea had a bell suspended over the grave with a wire leading down through the lid of the coffin, presumably into the hand of the person being buried. Apparently children of the era soon learnt how to scare the wits out of the neighbourhood by tying string to the bell wires and tugging at them from concealed vantage points.

In January 1979 the Conference of Medical Royal Colleges and Faculties of the U.K. produced a "Memorandum on the Diagnosis of Death."[9]

---

9 *Cadaveric Organs for Transplantation. A Code of Practice including Diagnosis of Brain Death. HMSO 1983. p.37.*

Paragraph 2 states: "Exceptionally, as a result of massive trauma, death occurs instantaneously or near-instantaneously. Far more commonly death is not an event, it is a process, the various organs and systems supporting the continuing of life failing and eventually ceasing altogether to function, successively and at different times."

In the chapter on resuscitation I described how a "dead" man's heart began to beat again. However, the irreversible damage to his brain and other organs meant that his life was over. All the hospital staff were doing was extending the period over which his entire system reached the point of irreversible collapse. I am told that it is often possible to detect dissociated electrical activity in a heart for 24 hours after death has been pronounced.

The usual sequence of system failure begins with the stopping of heartbeat or breathing, and ends with brain death. There are, however, occasions when the brain suffers severe damage, whether from a head injury or from bleeding within or around the brain. Here the normal order of events is reversed. Brain death results in the cessation of spontaneous breathing; and this is normally followed within minutes by cardiac arrest. However, it is, I am told, normal practice to support patients who have suffered an injury to their brain by taking over their breathing by means of a pulmonary ventilator — popularly referred to as a "life-support machine." This is to give the patient the best possible chance of recovery.

Only as it becomes clear that the brain damage has resulted in brain death does the function of the ventilator change imperceptibly from supporting life to extending dying. So long as the ventilator is oxygenating the blood the heartbeat can continue for some days, and for a time the blood flow will be adequate to maintain the function of other organs such as the liver and kidneys. The patient's chest rises and falls—just as it always did. He or she looks a healthy colour (pink if Caucasian)—just as he always did. Yet tests carried out on the functioning of the brain reveal that it has died. And if the brain has died, then the person has died, even though he may look healthier than the exhausted and heartbroken relatives at his bedside.

A farmer had fallen through the roof of a barn, landing on his head on the concrete floor below. He sustained massive head injuries and was transferred to a neurosurgical intensive care unit. Most of us are familiar with the swelling which follows bruising. The brain, however, is contained within the skull which will not yield to the pressure of the swelling brain. Instead, I am told, the brain tries to force its way down through the hole in the base of the skull through which the spinal cord passes. In extreme cases this can lead to tentorial herniation and the crushing of the brain stem, leading to brain death. This had happened to the farmer.

His wife was sitting beside his bed. The ventilator was doing his breathing, the cardiac monitor displayed his heartbeat. Yet she had been assured that he had died.

"What happens now?" she asked me.

I explained that there were two possibilities. The first was that, when she was ready, the ventilator would be disconnected, his breathing would stop at once, and after a few minutes his heart would also stop. She would be able to sit with him for as long as she wanted.

"Or?" she demanded. "You said there were two possibilities."

"Did your husband ever say anything about the idea of helping someone else have a better quality of life once he had died and no longer needed his body?"

"Oh! You're talking about organ donation. I was dreading that subject but didn't think it would be you who raised it."

"I only raised it because you asked. But if you are unhappy about it I'll make sure no-one else discusses it further with you. Consider the subject closed."

"But you can't approve of transplants."

"It doesn't matter what I think or approve. You are the only person whose opinion matters. And the only reason I would discuss it further is if it would help you to bring something positive out of this tragedy."

"But it doesn't say you can do transplants in the Bible."

"I'm not sure that the Bible was written with this kind of thing in mind, but are you sure of your facts?"

"Where does it say you can?"

"Do you recall that, in the second chapter of Genesis, the Lord is alleged to have caused a deep sleep to fall upon Adam, removed a rib, and from it created Eve?"

"Right," she said. "Where are the forms? I'll sign them!"

As it happens there is no legal necessity for the next of kin to sign any documents giving consent for donation of organs. It is sufficient that they have raised no objection.

Later that evening, when her husband had been taken to the operating theatre so that his liver and kidneys could be removed for donation, my discussion with the widow was being reported. The professor of surgery performing the operation commented that, so far as he was aware, at the stage of evolution in question, the only gas available to the Lord was methane, "and that's no good as an anaesthetic!"

Early in 1978 the Transplant Advisory Panel urged the United Kingdom Health Departments to consider producing a code of practice for procedures relating to the removal of organs for transplantation. A working party was set up to draft such a code for use by the staff involved. In February 1983 Her Majesty's Stationery Office published *Cadaveric Organs for Transplantation. A Code of Practice including Diagnosis of Brain Death.*

I was invited to sit in on a briefing for doctors, nurses, and administrative staff who might find themselves handling cases of brain death and organ donation. A member of the Working Party addressed the 30 or so of us. I was impressed at the care and expertise that had been brought to their work. Inevitably some of the technical neurophysiological details went over my head, but even I could follow how the five tests proposed to determine whether brain death had occurred made sense. At the end of a 40-minute presentation there was time for questions from the audience. Most were for clarification of technical points. The motivation for producing agreed tests for brain death had been the desire to increase the number of potential organs for donation. Gradually, as I absorbed the information we had been given, I found a question formulating in my mind. The member of the Working Party addressing us clearly dreaded having to field a question from a cleric. Eventually he could ignore my raised hand no longer. Although it was not a clinical test for brain death I enquired whether he would allow a sixth criterion for the conclusion that brain death had taken place, namely "The fact that the relatives tell *you* that the patient is dead. For unless they are convinced that he no longer needs the bits in his body you are never going to get their consent for the removal of those bits for transplantation." There was a moment of silence from the rostrum. Then there was a murmur of agreement from my colleagues in the audience as they changed gear from absorbing clinical data to engaging with the human and personal consequences of the diagnosis of brain death.

If death is generally a process in which the various organs and systems of my body fail and eventually cease altogether what happens to "me", my consciousness, my personality? Is there something which has been "me", expressed through my physical body during my lifetime which, upon my death, continues to exist but which is no longer confined in its expression to my body? Many cultures and religions have terms such as "spirit", "soul", "essence", "consciousness", "person", as well as "re-incarnation", "immortality", and more.

I was standing at the foot of the bed of a young man. The tests for brain death had just been carried out, and he fulfilled the criteria. Next to me stood the anaesthetist who, as he completed the tests noted the time of death.

"Where is he now?" he asked me, nodding at the body in the bed.

I ventured an opinion that he might well be nearby and aware of our concern for him. There is growing and serious research into the idea that consciousness is not restricted either by space or time. The issue behind Tony's question to me was addressed in the "Memorandum on the diagnosis of death":

"It is not difficult or illogical in any way to equate [the permanent and irreversible cessation of all functions of the brain] with the concept in many religions of the departure of the spirit from the body."[10]

On another occasion, following the removal of kidneys for donation, the body of a man was transferred from the operating theatre to the chapel of rest. I had arranged for his family to visit him there. His son produced his father's fishing hat, still adorned with several hooks and "flies". He asked if he could put it on Dad for a moment. He did, and there followed a light-hearted musing over the possibility that, somewhere in Europe, there might be a couple of recipients of his kidneys who suddenly and quite inexplicably developed an unprecedented obsession with fly-fishing! Hearsay and anecdotal reports suggest that facets of the donor's personality, tastes, and appetites may indeed be conveyed with the organ.[11] If, in years to come, this notion is substantiated I wonder whether there will have to be not only "tissue typing" but "personality typing" as well!

Since the recipients of organs are generally given only the most rudimentary information about the donor (e.g."male, mid 40s") they are unlikely to be able to extrapolate that he loved fly-fishing.

When families discovered, after the funerals of their children, that some organs had been retained for examination and research, they were desperately upset. The distress appeared to be that the grieving relatives, generally the parents, felt that not all of their child had been laid to rest. The inference was that he or she was thereby somehow

---

10 *Ibid. p.38.*

11 *"Paul Pearsall; The Heart's Code". Broadway Books, New York, p.83ff.*

prevented from being at peace, not least because the parents weren't at peace. Those who also had some hope of an after-life could find their distress compounded. "If she hasn't got all her organs and tissue she'll be incomplete in Heaven."

Very few students training to be clergy or ministers have much personal experience of bereavement. For them the academic doctrine of "the Resurrection of the Body" is just that — academic. The question "Shall I need all my bits in Heaven?" is therefore quite a challenge. If there is life beyond death, and if I shall have a discrete identity, rather than being part of an amorphous collective consciousness, then to what extent does that heavenly body depend on my earthly body? To the young and fit and healthy the prospect of eternity with such health and vigour may be attractive. As arthritis, deafness, and failing sight take their toll I am not so enamoured of the prospect of being a "crumbly" in Heaven. If academic theologically-trained minds have difficulty with the idea that their identities in Heaven are not dependent on their physical attributes on Earth, then it is no wonder that grieving people whose eyes are too full of tears to see the distant scene may presume that an incomplete earthly body results in an incomplete heavenly one.

There are others whose attitude towards their body and organ donation is strictly utilitarian and material. Following a rehearsal in the press of the arguments about opting in and opting out of being organ donors a correspondent wrote to me:

"Surely, as long as I am alive my body is mine, to be used as I may reasonably direct, but when I am dead, and it is no longer of any use to me, it should be transferable to anybody who has reasonable expectation of benefiting from it, and that regardless of any misguided prejudice which I may have in the matter."

In replying to him I drew on the experience of being called to a patient who, late at night, was fearful that he might die and that, against his wishes, his organs might be donated to others. I had been able to assure him that the Human Tissue Act 1961 provided for his concern. If he died in hospital the person "lawfully in possession of his body" would be the hospital administrator. He was permitted to authorise the removal of any part of the body for therapeutic purposes if, "having made such reasonable enquiry as may be practicable he had no reason to believe that the deceased had expressed an objection to his body being so dealt with after his death, and had not withdrawn it; or that the surviving spouse or any surviving relative of the deceased objects to the body being so dealt with."(1(2).)[12] After making a telephone call to the administrator I was able to reassure the patient that both the ward staff and the hospital administrator were aware of his objection.

My reply to my correspondent included:

"My experience of human beings — whether they be patients or staff in our health service — is that they are not motivated simply by "reason", however much they overlay their emotional response with the appearance of reason. A sick man in pain is a frightened man, and the cold logic that, upon his demise, he will not need his body is of no comfort to him unless he is already predisposed to the idea that he may be able to give others the chance of life.

To lie on one's deathbed, tired of living but scared of dying for fear that one may be dismembered and transplanted into strangers may be an irrational fear — but it is real."

---

12 *"Cadaveric Organs for Transplantation. A Code of Practice including Diagnosis of Brain Death."* HMSO 1983 p.30.

I suggest that any amendment to the Human Tissue Act, intended to increase the availability of organs and other tissue for transplantation, should take account of the non-rational fears of the sick.

There is a well meant but ill-advised comment which is made to the surviving relatives of an organ donor more often than I would wish. You are trying to grasp the momentous and unwelcome truth that your life's companion has died and will never be coming home again. Then you are told "Part of Jack is living on in someone else." At a physiological level it may be true that an organ which used to be in his body is now functioning in someone else's body. But the cells which made up Jack's liver (say) two years ago are not the same cells as it comprised last week when it was transplanted. And none of the cells of his liver which was lifted carefully out of his body upon his death will still exist in another two years' time. Most cells in our body are, I am assured, being constantly replaced. At the physiological level, therefore, the statement is not very accurate.

At the psychological level it can be disastrous. "If you say that part of him is living on in someone else then I can't say that I have laid him to rest, since part of him wasn't buried last week." This obstructs the process of "letting go" which is necessary for a healthy resolution of grief. Secondly what happens if the donated liver is subsequently rejected or the recipient dies? The family can suffer a double bereavement as a bit more of Jack dies. A third problem arises if Jack's widow latches on to the notion that she has a proprietary interest in the recipient of the donated organ. Although she is unlikely ever to discover the identity of the recipient she may conjure up a scenario in which the recipient "owes" it to her to live responsibly — to look after Jack's liver for him (and her). This can seem particularly important if she imagines that the recipient's own liver had failed as a consequence of alcohol abuse.

For any and all of these reasons transplant teams discourage comments like this.

One of the theological students whom I mentioned earlier had a specific concern about the diagnosis of brain death and the transplanting of donated organs. "Isn't there something of playing God — of deciding who shall live and who shall die?"

My reply to him was "Come and see."

We went to an intensive care bay where a teenager had suffered head injuries in a road traffic accident. The consultant in charge of the lad was about to carry out the first set of tests to determine whether his brain had died. My student was given a full and detailed explanation of what was done, and why. At the end of this examination, which took nearly an hour, I asked the student if he felt the surgeon was playing God. He had seen a senior doctor using all his skills to admit defeat. As a neurosurgeon there was nothing more he could do for the lad. As a father of young children of his own he hurt. There was nothing in his expression or manner to suggest he considered himself divine. The student admitted that here there had been no trace of playing at being God.

Later he accompanied the lad to the operating theatre for organ donation, along with the staff nurse who had been caring for him. As the theatre doors closed and we were left outside we felt like we were in Hell — a place not normally associated with God. Later that evening the student accompanied me and the lad's family to the chapel of rest so that they could say farewell. Again, no trace of human beings playing at being God. He saw what is normally kept from the public gaze. The staff nurse who, having taken her patient to theatre for organ donation, buried her head in my shoulder and sobbed "There's just too much grief."

> "Death is only conclusively established when the [brain death] criteria have been satisfied on two successive occasions. As a patient must be presumed to be alive until it is clearly established that he is dead, the time of death should be recorded as the time when death was conclusively established, not some earlier time or a later time when artificial ventilation is withdrawn or the heartbeat ceases." (Code of Practice, paragraph 30).[13]

One of the tests carried out to determine whether the brain is dead involves disconnecting the ventilator to see if there is any hint of spontaneous breathing. If the patient is subsequently to be taken to theatre for organ donation the ventilator is reconnected.

If, however, organ donation is not proposed there are two possible scenarios. Upon completion of the second set of tests the ventilator may be left disconnected. There is no spontaneous breathing, the heartbeat slows down, becomes erratic, and stops. The patient's colour changes, there may be some body movement for a few seconds, and then all becomes still. The ventilator, cardiac monitor and other equipment may be removed so as to provide the family with more space at the bedside.

Alternatively the ventilator may be reinstated so that relatives who may have had to travel some distance can get to the bedside and take their leave before it is disconnected for the last time.

---

13 *Ibid. p.12.*

In one case a young husband requested specifically that he be at his wife's side when the ventilator was finally disconnected.   The   consultant   and   the   staff   nurse "specialling" him agreed. Although I had read the passage in the Code of Practice relating to "Integrity of Spinal Reflexes" I was not prepared for what followed. "It is well established that spinal-cord function can persist after insults which irretrievably destroy brain-stem function. Reflexes of spinal origin may persist or return after an initial absence in brain dead patients."[14]   The ventilator was disconnected. The heartbeat began to slow down and just as it stopped the young woman sat up. Her arms reached out in front of her, the palms of her hands facing away from each other. The staff nurse and I shared a glance of wide-eyed panic. She later admitted to having a momentary fear that the brain death tests might not have been accurate.   Then, as the spinal reflexes wore off, the patient fell back on to her pillows and lay still. We were greatly reassured by her husband who had been beside her throughout.

"That wasn't my Melanie. She never moved like that."

For all that the movement was dramatic and distressing it served to help Melanie's husband take in the truth that she was no longer alive.

Sometimes when the family has been present at the final disconnection of the ventilator they speak of feeling guilty. They have said when they are ready, and the ventilator is turned   off.   This,   they   feel,   is   their   decision,   their responsibility, even their fault, that now their patient has died.

---

14 *Ibid. p.35.*

It is difficult to find the right way to reassure them, especially since feelings of guilt, of "if only", are typical at such times. I try to point out that the decision whether to turn off the ventilator is one which has to be taken by the doctor. He/she will decide whether the ventilator is supporting life or extending dying.

They are being invited to indicate when they are ready, insofar as they ever will be, to take their leave. No-one will burden them with responsibility for the decision *whether* to turn off, only to declare the timing *when*.

A little girl, her parents, and brother were all injured in a car crash caused by a drunken doctor. Kayley suffered severe damage to her spine and brain. She was in the paediatric intensive care unit. Her parents were on a ward two floors above, and her brother was on the children's ward on the floor below her. The decision whether to turn off the ventilator had been made once brain death had been established. Her parents could not move to be with us on the unit, and so we decided to put her in a dress and bonnet and take her up to them so that they could cuddle her before we transferred her to the mortuary. Her grandparents and close family wanted to be with her when the ventilator was turned off. It had been agreed that the traffic police officer who was investigating the case be present in order to provide continuity of evidence. The consultant checked that everyone was ready, and just as he was about to disconnect the airway Kayley's grandfather said "I get the impression that this death is being managed."

The police officer told me later that this had caused him a moment of anxiety until I responded by asking "Does that cause you a problem?"

To this Grandad replied "No. I think it's bloody marvellous!"

The nurse carried Kayley and I carried an oxygen cylinder and face mask (which were intended to deceive inquisitive onlookers) up to her parents. Meanwhile the police officer took her grandparents and extended family down to the hospital chapel where they wanted some peace and quiet.

Sometimes the patient who is thought to be brain-dead does not wait for the tests to be carried out. The heartbeat becomes unstable and stops on its own while the ventilator is still connected. After one such instance the neurologist told me with mock gravity that the patient "had chosen the medieval way to die."

Although transplant co-ordinators ensure the privacy both of donor families and the recipients of donated organs they have been ready, in my experience, to forward letters of thanks from recipients. One such person asked me to help her compose a letter of thanks to the donor of her new liver. I was taken aback by the wording of her request but tried not to show it.

"Do you have a mental picture of who is going to receive your letter?" I asked. "Could it be the surviving partner of a long and fulfilled marriage, or the heartbroken parents of a teenager?"

Her jaw dropped. It had not occurred to her that the gift of her new liver had come at such a high price—the death of its donor. It took us half an hour to address this fact before we could even begin the letter. I hope the family receiving it were able to take comfort that something positive— embodied in a healthy and grateful recipient—had been retrieved from what was otherwise an unmitigated tragedy.

There are some doctors who are unable to accept that the brain death tests are evidence of the irreversible end of life. For them, as long as the heart is beating and the lungs are being inflated, albeit by a mechanical and external means (a ventilator), the patient is alive. As a consequence they will not take part in the removal of organs from what they consider to be "live" patients.

I am assured that there have been no cases anywhere in the world of someone whose brain has been found to have died subsequently reviving. A story was syndicated to five English national daily newspapers in 1990. Allegedly, "astonished doctors saw [the patient's] tongue move six hours after he had been pronounced brain-dead." At no stage had the patient fulfilled the criteria for the establishment of brain death. His subsequent "amazing recovery" owed everything to the first-class care he was given by the team in the neurosurgical unit. The staff had called me to support the family after his condition had deteriorated. One of the relatives told me, quite understandably, "You're no use here if you can't do a miracle." It was a point I did not contest. Eight hours later, as the crisis appeared to have passed, the same relative somewhat sheepishly took my hand and said "Thank you. The miracle has worked!"

The story would probably not have been taken up by so many national newspapers had it been reported accurately: "Critically ill patient receives first-rate care and makes full recovery."

I am told that some journalists thrive on the adage "Why let the facts spoil a good story?" The trouble was that the story, as it appeared, called into question the reliability of the tests for brain death. It sowed doubt in the minds of people who carried organ donor cards, and of families being approached when their relatives had fulfilled the brain death criteria. The professor of surgery told me the day after these newspaper reports appeared that all of Europe's transplant programmes had ground to a halt as a consequence. In the days following this inaccurate and irresponsible reporting I heard several occasions on which the terms "brain-dead" and "journalist" were used in the same sentence! I am grateful to another journalist, Tony Scase, who saw the ethical and clinical implications of his professional colleague's behaviour and did a piece on television to put the record straight. The neurosurgeon responsible for the care of the patient in question is on record as saying "In no case has any patient who has been through the set of tests and fulfilled the criteria for brain death ever recovered."

Woody Allen's view on death is reported to be that he doesn't want to be there when it happens. Since most of us lose consciousness well before our hearts finally stop, he and we are likely to achieve that aspiration.

God's fool

A young patient noticed me working on a children's ward. I was not wearing theatre "greens", and so I couldn't be a surgeon, Instead of a stethoscope round my neck I wore a clerical collar, and so I couldn't be a physician. I was not wearing nurse's uniform, but I was wearing a home-made badge such as all other staff on the ward wore. As the female staff's badges declared them to be "Aunty Julie"(say), so mine defined me as "Uncle Ian". It was a source of amusement in the local supermarket checkout when it was noticed that on one occasion I had forgotten to remove my badge after work.

The boy asked a nurse who I was.

"That's Uncle Ian."

"What does he do?"

"Uncle Ian? He's the man who talks to God."

Apparently it was stated in such a matter-of-fact way that the young inquisitor accepted the answer he had been given without further comment.

The hospital chaplain's role, both as to what we *are* and also what we *do,* is hard to define in single words. There are those who, probably masking their own political agendas, claim that the Health Service can do without them since they have no role in a post-religious age. Those who go in for religion, they claim, can call in their own priests, pastors, etc.

Within any institution there are politics — people with a status to maintain, targets of throughput to achieve, budgets to control. All of this is while riding on the public fantasy that nurses are angels and doctors know best. I am told that in the medieval court there was one character above all others who was trusted by the king. He had no political axe to grind, no craving for a dukedom or estates or wealth. He moved freely through all the strata of court life. He heard the distress of the marginalised, the machinations of the ambitious, and the flatulence of the pompous. The court jester was the one person whom the king could rely upon to be unbiased. As the Clown he was probably the only member of court who could tell the king he was a prat without having his head chopped off. In my experience the image of court jester rings true for much of hospital chaplaincy. God's Fool speaks of hope in the face of disaster, of life in the presence of death, of love where there is ample evidence of hatred. Quite a few members of staff in a hospital, as in the medieval court, have agendas of their own, some of which they cannot admit even to themselves. Any jester who dares to hold up a mirror for them to see themselves as the rest of us see them is likely to be resented.

On the other hand God's Fool is also a "safe person'"whom others search out to provide a listening ear or for advice. This is because that counsel is presumed to be unbiased, and because it will be given in confidence. However he is not isolated from the system. He is part of it and is affected by it. Like Canio in the opera *Pagliacci*, there are times when he is required to carry on with the show even when his own heart is breaking.

God's Fool may occasionally have a role in breaking the cycle of tension and stress with humour. It is risky. It may backfire, and the chaplain may be accused of being facetious or, as I have been, of showing a "lack of *gravitas*". The dark humour of the Armed Forces and Emergency Services, often misunderstood by outsiders, may be the contemporary equivalent of the medieval court jester's activity.

Psychoanalyst Mart Grotjahn notes that "To have a sense of humor is to have an understanding of human suffering and misery. Humor bespeaks a sad acceptance of our weakness and frustration. But laughter also means freedom."[15]

I had spent most of a long and sad night on the Delivery Unit, moving from one couple to another after late miscarriages or stillbirth. At about 5.30am. we were sitting at the nurses' station comforting ourselves with coffee and chocolate biscuits. While his mother had a shower one healthy babe was being cuddled by the midwife who had delivered him. Another midwife returned to the nurses' station and looked over the shoulder of her colleague at the newborn baby.

"Ooh!" said Di. "It makes me feel all broody. Ian, can you spare a minute?"

Amid the laughter all I could think of by way of rejoinder was "Oh! Only a minute?"

Christmas Eve had been particularly traumatic in Accident and Emergency. There had been a house fire in which people had died. I had spent much of the night supporting relatives as they identified the bodies. One little girl had survived and was being monitored in A.& E. after inhaling smoke. The police sergeant in charge of the investigation was upset that she had no daddy, no brother, no home, no toys. He nipped home and came back with a little fluffy toy white kitten to give her as a Christmas present. As we stood in the corridor outside her room I could see the muscles in his jaw tensing before he went in to give her the toy.

"How do I get him to relax and be the Dutch uncle he wants to be for her?" I thought. Having spent hours working with him in the mortuary and chapel of rest I took a chance.

---

15 "Beyond Laughter: Humor and the Subconscious." New York: McGraw-Hill, 1957.

I turned to him and said "You know why the Christmas story had to happen in Bethlehem?"

He clenched his fists and teeth and muttered "Don't you bloody talk religion after what we've been through!"

I smiled and replied "It had to happen in Bethlehem because it wasn't possible to find three wise men or any virgins in E-- (I named a county in the South East of England)."

He slid down the wall and ended up in a heap of giggles on the floor. *Then* he was in a fit state to take his gift in to the little girl.

In the ground-floor day room of a psychiatric intensive care unit the charge nurse was telling me of a patient who was convinced that he was the Archangel Gabriel. Mischievously I said "What makes you so sure he's not?"

He looked at me as if to say "You're beyond redemption!" when we both heard running footsteps in the room above us. There was an almighty crash as the aforesaid patient went through the window, landed on the ground outside the day room, and trotted off. As we set off in a pincer movement to retrieve him I called out "See what I mean?"

Some years after retiring I was taking a break from platform duties at a miniature steam railway. Sitting in the clubhouse with members of my family I was enjoying a cup of tea when a woman came in and asked if I worked at the hospital. I replied that I used to.

"You were the chaplain, weren't you?"

"Yes."

"You helped my husband and me when our twin boys died."

Her name and the details came back to me. Knowing that her parents, who spoke no English, were coming from Italy for the funeral I had enlisted the help of an Italian doctor in translating one of the prayers into Italian and then coaching me in pronouncing the words correctly.

"I thought it was you but since you are not wearing a priest's clothes I wasn't sure until I heard you laugh."

I cannot remember how we had managed laughter in the context of her babies' death, but we obviously had. Furthermore her recollection of my laugh was a positive thing—something by which she was happy to remember me.

The hospital chaplain's contract (at least in my case) requires that he/she provide for the spiritual and pastoral care of patients, relatives, and staff. Since I suspect that no two of us share the same understanding of "spiritual" or "pastoral" care it is as well that the terms are not more precisely defined. It does, however, mean that staff of all grades and disciplines have a right of access to us. I have been told that the hospital chaplain has this in common with the naval chaplain, that he has no rank of his own. He derives his rank from the person he is with. For so long as I am sitting on the floor in the hospital incinerator unit keeping the operator company while the Fire Brigade devise a way of freeing him from a piece of equipment which has trapped him I have the rank of incinerator operator. I am equally comfortable sharing the chief executive's coffee while he outlines some aspect of hospital trust strategy or concern he has for a colleague. The chaplain has also been described as the one person in the hospital it is safe to scream at without it affecting your promotion prospects. On one occasion a nurse stormed into my office and exclaimed "Sit down, shut up, and listen. I've got to winge!" So I did, and she did.

The switchboard patched a call through to me at 12.45 one night. The operator had noticed the distress in the caller's voice. It was a senior doctor. He told me that he was going to kill himself. Knowing him and the area in which he worked I realized that he had access to the means of doing so. At least he was talking, and so I kept him talking. For two and a half hours he talked. Then he summed up his exhaustion and dejection by reading to me the epitaph he had written for himself. "He cared. But in today's N.H.S. care is not enough. It knows the cost of everything and the value of nothing."

After a moment of silence I said "Do you want me to quote that to your family, your colleagues, and the coroner when I take them to the chapel of rest in the morning to identify your body? Or do you want to tell them yourself?"

"Damn you, Ian! I'll tell them myself!"

He is alive, working, and has given me permission to recount this.

Those who, for whatever reason, consider that the money spent on hospital chaplains' salaries (0.15% of the N.H.S. budget at my last enquiry) would be better used to employ, say, more nurses, deserve a reasoned and unprejudiced rejoinder. As with many occupations in the public services sector the difficulty lies in finding an appropriate yardstick by which to measure chaplains' "worth". One suggestion for determining the cost benefit of hospital chaplains is "Do people feel better for their involvement?" When a member of parliament said he thought this was somewhat ephemeral, I responded by enquiring what criterion he would accept in cost-benefit analysis for M.P.s. The subject was promptly dropped!

Mary described herself as a paraplegic burnt-out schizophrenic. Most of her adult life had been spent in a psychiatric institution. She would cajole people to wheel her to the hospital chapel for services where she would try to engage me in discussion on the philosophy of religion. I say "try" because I think she found my ignorance of the subject lamentable. She was transferred to a surgical ward after she began to lose blood from both ends of her alimentary tract. The surgeon presumed that she would want corrective surgery. He ordered that blood be cross-matched and that she be transfused. Mary objected. She insisted that her life was over. She would never walk. Her mental condition was such that she would never lead an independent life. She had no relatives. With some vigour she told me "Stop messing about!" The junior house officer was bewildered. He took his instructions from the consultant, yet this patient was refusing what he thought would be the welcome offer of life-saving surgery. In the end I spoke with the surgeon on the telephone. He asked if she realised that, without surgery, she would die.

"Yes," I replied.

"Could I get her sectioned [detained under a section of the Mental Health Act on the grounds that she is incapable of making competent decisions about her treatment]?"

"I doubt it," I replied. "She is more lucid and realistic about her future than I've ever known her, but for a competent opinion you'll need to talk with the psychiatrist in charge of her care." I think the prospect of doing this so alarmed him that he took my word for it. It was agreed that Mary's view would be respected. Blood would not be "wasted" on her (her term, not ours). She would not be subjected to surgery. All that she asked was that I stay with her until she died.

We moved her into a single room, and the nursing staff found me an armchair as I prepared for a long night. She drifted off to sleep at about 10pm. At one o'clock she awoke. She was very pale and beads of perspiration were trickling down her face. The staff had been reluctant to change the soiled linen for fear of disturbing her, but she now agreed to let them do this. I then returned to my vigil beside the bed.

"What's the noise?" she demanded.

"Describe it to me."

"A hissing, high pitched whistle."

"I can't hear it," I replied. "It may be the consequence of your lack of blood — producing a sort of singing in your ears. Is it troubling you?"

"Not particularly."

She drifted off to sleep again, stirred at about 4am, and died at six.

The staff felt better for my involvement. On a busy surgical ward they would have had difficulty allocating one nurse to sit with Mary all night. The idea of being with someone who knew that her refusal of surgery would result in her death was pretty challenging. Furthermore the smell in the room was offensive.

One of the traditional duties of a hospital chaplain is to share the bread and wine of the Holy Communion with those patients to whom this is important. I had been called, early one Saturday morning, to one such patient. On arrival on the ward I sensed a very hostile atmosphere. An enquiring look at the night sister resulted in her beckoning me into her office. There she explained the reason. The ward was a female surgical one, with fifteen beds down each side. During the night a woman had been admitted. She was haemorrhaging after attempting to procure an abortion using a knitting needle. Her crying and moaning had kept most of the other patients awake. Since some of them were trying to rest in an attempt to prevent miscarriages the grounds for conflict were considerable. I was taken to the bedside of the person who had asked to receive Communion. She was clearly tired but seemed to bear no grudge against the cause of her lack of sleep who lay in the bed opposite. The curtains were drawn round her. We shared the Sacrament, and I drew back the curtains again. From the bed opposite came a loud and strident cry.

"You must think I'm the filthiest sinner alive."

Taken aback, I took a breath, steadied myself against the foot of the bed of the patient I had been visiting, and said quietly "Does it matter what I think of you?"

The distraught woman clearly interpreted my non-judgemental response as her cue to make a full and public confession which left nothing to the imagination and every eye on the ward fixed on her. The day staff were arriving and stopped in their tracks. The breakfast trolley seemed to skid to a halt, and even the cornflakes on it might have been curling up in embarrassment.

When she had finished I said "I seem to remember something like this happening some years ago. Then some of the town's most respectable leaders dragged a lass in your position in front of a popular preacher who had turned up. They told him that they had caught her in the act of adultery, for which, at the time, the penalty was death.

What was he going to do about her? The preacher started doodling in the dust on the ground with his finger, and then said casually that he supposed that anyone who had never done anything wrong might as well start throwing stones at her. One by one the worthy gentlemen slunk away, since most of them had had a bit on the side at some time. Eventually there was no-one left—just the poor lass and the preacher. Jesus looked up at her and said 'Isn't there anyone with a clear conscience left to condemn you? Well then, neither do I condemn you. Goo you on, gal' he say. 'Goo you on, an' doon't you do that noo more!' " (The patient was from North Norfolk).

Suddenly, as I finished the story[16] the tension collapsed. The ward staff cleared their throats and busied themselves getting the breakfast trolley moving. I gave the woman a hug and left.

Later in the day I looked back on the ward. The sister in charge couldn't wait to tell me how much the atmosphere had changed. Every patient, she told me, who could get out of bed had done so and had made their way, one at a time, to the focus of the previous night's resentment. They had sat with her, commiserated with her, and made their peace with her. It could be claimed that there were 30 people, not counting the ward staff, who felt better for the chaplain's involvement.

One Sunday evening, on another surgical ward, a woman was being visited by her husband. As a nurse passed by she heard the man asking his wife if she had received Holy Communion that day. On hearing that she hadn't, the nurse apologised for eavesdropping and enquired whether she might call the chaplain.

16 *Gospel of John, chapter 8.*

Since I was already in the hospital it was only a matter of minutes before I joined the couple, just as visiting time was ending. The husband asked if he could stay and share Communion with his wife. She suggested that he went to ring home in order to explain to the children that he would be slightly later than planned. While he was doing this she told me that she wanted to "travel light" to major surgery the next day. To this end she asked me to help her make her confession. She completed this private task and her husband returned. We celebrated the Eucharist together. Just as we had finished the nurse returned and hung a notice on the foot of the bed "Patient fasting for theatre."

"Bit like the Last Supper!" said the woman.

The couple had outlined to me the nature of the proposed operation. It seemed entirely understandable that she was apprehensive. She said that she was afraid she might let the side down and get panicky in the morning. I reminded her that the physiotherapist had encouraged her to do breathing exercises. If, as she breathed slowly and steadily, she thought the word "Jesus" while breathing out, she would turn even her breathing into a prayer. She tried it and found that it made sense. She then asked if I would accompany her to theatre the next morning to remind her about the breathing. As her husband and I left the ward he thanked me for agreeing to do so.

To start with the next morning she did not recognise me in theatre "greens" helping the theatre porter transfer her from her bed on to the trolley. In the anaesthetic room I held one of her hands when the anaesthetist took the other.

"Just a little scratch in the back of your hand," he said.

"You lying toad, Jimmy," I thought as I watched the needle going into her vein.

"Do your breathing—slowly in—and, as you breathe out, just think that name," I said. I saw her lips moving with the word "Jesus," and then her eyelids flickered, and she was away.

"Hey, Ian! What the hell have you done?" Jimmy said. "Someone her weight needs 40 mls, and she's out with 20."

Years later, in a different hospital, I had arrived, as scheduled and on time for once, on a medical ward to bring the Holy Communion to a patient one Sunday morning. She was attached to a cardiac monitor. As the staff nurse and I reached the bed she noticed evidence on the monitor of ventricular tachycardia. This is when the pulse gets very fast. I gather that it can lead to a point when the heart stops beating properly and, instead, flutters in ventricular fibrillation. The staff nurse asked me to stay with the patient while she ran to get a doctor. He took one look at the monitor and called out the crash team. I backed off. People pushing crash trolleys at speed are something of a danger to those in their path. The patient called to me "I want my Communion."

The doctor looked at the monitor, at the patient, and then said "How quick can you be?"

"90 seconds," I replied, more in hope than with confidence.

"We'll wait. She needs the Sacrament."

The mental and spiritual gymnastics required to maintain some semblance of devotion and calm were considerable. Outside the curtains surrounding the bed I could hear the wail of crash bleeps, running feet, subdued but urgent voices, some clearly out of breath. Most of the 90 seconds were taken up with the patient clinging to my hand after receiving the bread and wine. I got up from kneeling beside her bed and drew back the curtains. There we both saw the entire team ready to pounce. Except that they didn't. The registrar pointed at the monitor and said "She's back in sinus rhythm. Ian, you must do this more often!"

I do not imagine that people felt any less helpless two thousand years ago than they do today when sitting beside the bed of a loved one who is dying. It would therefore be no surprise to me if it could be demonstrated that the early Christian Church devised the service called the "Sacrament of the Sick" or "Anointing" primarily as a response to the sense of helplessness, of "wishing there was something we could do". It was in such a context that a dying woman's son said just that : "If only there was something we could do."

Somewhat diffidently I explained to the gathered family, who gave me no indication of familiarity with "churchy" matters, that there was a brief and simple service which had been devised for occasions like this. They pressed me to give more details. I explained that, long before today's medicines for pain relief and sedation, highly refined olive oil, sometimes with expensive perfumes added, was applied to the fevered brow. It seemed to help the patient feel comfortable and it provided a focus for the longing of all those in the room for the peace and well-being of the sick person. Adding my own gloss on the symbolism I said that I liked to think that it also oiled the hinges of the gates of Heaven so as to smooth the dying person's journey home.

I sat quietly at the bedside while the eight or so members of the unconscious woman's family absorbed and then discussed my comments. After a while they were agreed that they would like me to "do this service" for Mother. Since they had told me earlier how much they had valued the care of one of the nurses who was looking after their mother I enquired if they would like me to invite her to join us if her duties allowed. They were keen that she be with them. I went and found her, outlined what was proposed, and invited her to join us. Having never seen this before she was hesitant but inquisitive. The ward sister encouraged her, especially since the family had been explicit in their invitation. The idea that the oil had been set aside especially for this purpose by the local bishop — not just poured out of a bottle from the kitchen — added to the sense that we were engaged in something special for and with Mother. After the briefest of prayers, in which we asked that God's love be ahead of her to guide her, beneath her to support her, above her to protect her, and behind her to defend her, we assured her of our love. I used the oil to make a sign of the Cross on her forehead. Each member of her family gave her a kiss, and we tip-toed out of the room. It was the nurse who observed that the service seemed to give the family permission to leave. I added that perhaps it was also giving the patient permission to leave. It is well known that the sense of hearing persists even when the other senses have shut down.

Later that evening I visited the woman's home. We had been told that the family would stay there awaiting news. Rather than tell them over the telephone that Mother had died it seemed more personal to call. The son's comment to me was "You shouldn't have been shy at offering us that service. It helped a lot."

It was a quarter to midnight when my bleep went off. I rang the hospital and spoke to a consultant anaesthetist.

"Can you come?" she asked. "I have a patient who will die if we don't operate tonight, but she refuses to give consent until she's made her confession."

Twenty minutes after being woken up I was in the theatre suite. The anaesthetist explained that the patient had a strangulated hernia which had been so deprived of blood that the gut was dying and poisoning her. Worse still she had severely high blood pressure and was overweight — all of which added up to her being a high risk. Armed with this gloomy picture I was taken to be with the patient. The area was cleared so that we were not overheard, and she sought the assurance of God's forgiveness.

"Be at peace," I concluded. "God has put away your sins. The truest thing about you is that you are loved."

"Could you stay with me until I am asleep?" she asked.

"Of course," I replied. "And I promise to be here after the operation is complete." I chose my words carefully since I had been told that she might die on the table. However, I felt it was important for her to know that I would not desert her, whatever the outcome.

The theatre team reassembled. We wheeled her trolley into the anaesthetic room. I sat on a stool beside her while the anaesthetist helped her drift off to sleep. It took six of us to lift her on to the operating table. I was about to leave when the anaesthetist said "I don't know what you've done, Ian. But her blood pressure is back down within the normal range."

It was agreed that I would be bleeped when the operation was over. I changed out of theatre "greens" into my usual "clericals" and went up to the ward to find the woman's son. He had been aware that I was involved and was glad to hear his mother was relaxed as she went to sleep. He seemed to want company and so we walked in the hospital grounds in the dark. A couple of hours later my bleep went off with a message to ring Theatres. We returned to the switchboard. My mouth was dry with apprehension. The news was good. The surgery had been successful, and the patient was being wheeled into Recovery. I relayed this to her son and invited him to return to the ward where I would join him when I helped bring Mother back up there. I returned to Theatres, changed again into the shapeless "greens" and "J cloth" mob-cap, and sat once again beside the sleeping patient. After a short while she came round. She looked up at me — the same face that she had seen as she had gone to sleep. In a bleary voice she said "You look dead glam!"

The theatre staff promptly put me back in my place by pointing out that anyone would need to be pretty well doped to say that of me! The patient made a good recovery.

I have described how a child was told that I was the "man who talked to God." An adult, seeing me in the hospital, said "Ah! So you're the Maker's Rep., are you?"

I like those descriptions. Not only am I supposed to commend the Maker and His product to doubtful consumers. I am also expected to convey the comments, complaints, and requests of customers back to Headquarters. Whether you call that "talking to God" or "prayer", it is what chaplains may reasonably be expected to do.

Until someone can produce a better criterion for assessing the cost benefit of hospital chaplains I shall continue with "Do people feel better for their involvement?"

The Five T's of bereavement first aid

The annual review of the Registrar General on deaths in England and Wales in 2000, published by the Office of National Statistics, reported that 66.5% took place in hospital, 4.3% in hospices, and 7.8% in other communal establishments. In other words 78.6% did *not* take place at home.

It is also a matter of public record that more people are living to a greater age and therefore drawing pensions for longer than ever before. If you had been growing up in Liverpool at the start of the 20th century I am told that you could have expected that, by the time you were 21 years old, half your peer group would have died.

Within a century in Britain the patterns of bereavement have changed significantly. Whether it is the "institutionalisation of death" (in hospitals rather than at home), the relatively new phenomenon that many people do not experience bereavement until they themselves are pensioners, or the alleged decline in awareness of one's neighbours — whether it is the consequence of one or more of these factors, people seem ill prepared for bereavement. Death has been described as "the last taboo." Apparently we can discuss sex, religion, and politics, but not death.

What can be done to minimise the sense of loneliness and isolation of the bereaved? How can it be made easier for them to grasp the reality of the death, not just intellectually but emotionally, so that they can begin to move forward? Bereavement counselling and therapy are frequently offered when people are thought to be failing to "get over it". Were there everyday mechanisms which people used at the beginning of the 20th century which we might do well to employ at the beginning of the 21st?

When the majority of deaths took place at home, and before undertakers advertised their "complete funeral service," physical contact with the body of the person who had died was commonplace. The practicalities of closing the eyes and mouth, of cleaning up after the final relaxation of bladder and bowel—such "last offices" were labours of love carried out by members of the family, possibly with assistance from neighbours familiar with such tasks. They involved touch.

The flow of neighbours calling to pay their respects meant that the family had repeated opportunities to talk about the circumstances of their bereavement.

The shedding of tears of grief was apparently much more widespread than the term "stiff upper lip" would lead us to believe.

Before the days of central heating it was normal for there to be standing on a trivet in the hearth beside the open fire a kettle full of water ready for the provision of tea for visitors.

Finally, time could be spent in the front parlour with Grandma where she lay in her open coffin before the funeral. Such time, at the time of bereavement, may have been more significant than we give credit.

These simple, practical, and natural phenomena of Touch, Talking, Tears, Tea, and Time—what I have called The Five T's of bereavement First Aid—seem to help the newly bereaved.

Bereavement first aid: Touch

As a child you woke up frightened by thunder or a nightmare. The best comfort generally is to be hugged, to be reassured that, however shocked or frightened you have been, you are awake, alive, safe, and cared for. Adults, shocked by good news as well as by bad, often need physical contact to confirm that they are "in touch" with reality, that they are awake, and that this is not a dream. I have been told of a student nurse who was woken by the postman delivering the results of her final examinations. She stumbled out of bed, opened the letter, discovered that she had passed, ran out into the road and, in her pyjamas, hugged the postman who lost his balance, so that they and his bicycle all ended up in a heap in the road!

There are many people familiar with the dictum "I needed to pinch myself to make sure I was awake." When the nightmare is that someone you love has just died it is entirely reasonable that your first reaction is one of denial: "No! There must be some mistake." Within the constraints necessary to avoid accusations of inappropriate physical contact a hand held or an arm around a shoulder are non-verbal ways of steadying someone when the news has thrown them off balance. The companionship of another human being as you try to absorb the news delivered by a police officer that your son has been found dead — a hand to hold, eyes to peer into, searching for any evidence that this is, after all, a sick joke, someone to hug you while you shake with shock — the touch of human kindness in those first moments not only makes the nightmare marginally more bearable, but it also provides a safe environment for you to take in the implications of that devastating news and to stay connected with reality. If you are someone who prefers not to have your hand held or to be hugged your tensing or avoiding such contact should give a clear message to your companion that the physical contact is not welcome.

Touch seems to be important in another way. The bereaved families of the 51 people who died in the *Marchioness* disaster complained that they had been prevented by an officer on the coroner's staff from seeing or touching their bodies. Their frustration and anguish is a matter of public record.[17]

To be able to hold the hand of your life's partner, to register that it is still, unresponsive, and getting cool — this is worth more than a thousand recitations of the mantra "There, there, dear! You remember him like he was." Sometimes the damage to the body is so great that it is genuinely impossible to hold a hand. Mortuary staff and funeral directors can sometimes provide other ways for direct contact, enabling the bereaved to "grasp'"the reality. When a body had been so badly burnt that the wedding ring fell off the ring finger the mortuary technician logged the ring as valuable property. He then placed it on the clean white sheet covering the remains of the body. When I took the spouse to the chapel of rest it was the ring, with its unusual engraving, which provided the focus for tenderness and tears.
Held in the palm of the hand the ring was kissed and spoken to as if it now formed the remaining essence of the partner. Leave taking was achieved, the ring was replaced on the

---

17 *A riverboat on the Thames which was hit and sunk by a dredger on 20 August, 1989. On 30 November, 2000 Lord Justice Clark opened a Non-Statutory Inquiry into the identification of victims of the Marchioness disaster following mutilation (severing of hands) on the orders of the Coroner for the purposes of identification, and complaints by relatives that they had been prevented from viewing the bodies of the victims.*

sheet covering the chest of the victim, and the spouse was able to "let go".

Following a particularly traumatic accident the driver of a vehicle was decapitated and then enveloped in flames. His wife was urged not to see him but to "remember him as he was". The recommendation was unfortunate because she had seen photographs of his smouldering remains. Her most recent memories of him were therefore traumatic and distressing. It was reported to me that she was in no doubt about his death but that there were "things she needed to say to him."

I conferred with the mortuary technician and the coroner's pathologist. We were able to relocate the man's head on his shoulders and to straighten out his limbs. His left foot was undamaged and so we devised a way of enabling it to be visible while the rest of him lay under a sheet. I made contact with his wife and explained what we could offer. She accepted, and her father-in-law brought her to the chapel of rest. He was very angry with me. He felt we were going to make it far worse for her, and that, instead she ought to remember him as he was. I explained that he did not have to see his son.[18] He was welcome to stay in the sitting-room adjacent to the chapel of rest. I explained to his daughter-in-law that I had put a chair for her at the foot of the catafalque on which her husband lay. He was completely covered but she would be able to see his outline under the sheet. If she wanted I would uncover his left foot for her.

We went in to be with her husband. She felt his head, shoulders, chest, waist, groin, thighs, and legs and then sat down. I uncovered his left foot. She took it in her hands,

---

18 *No one can be compelled to identify a dead body.*

kissed his toes, and tickled his instep. "This always used to drive him wild!" she explained to me. Choking back my own tears I thought "You have shared with me intimate details of your private life. But you have, by this uniquely personal means, provided yourself with tangible evidence that this is your husband and that he is no longer alive."

She held his cold foot against her cheek and rocked gently back and forth. After ten minutes she kissed his toes once more and tucked his foot up as if settling one of their children down for the night. She then stood up and told me "Today's our seventh wedding anniversary." As I took her back to join her father-in-law I thought how near we had been to failing to allow her to acknowledge this anniversary. Her father-in-law expected that she would be a gibbering wreck of emotion. Instead she was walking tall. He did a complete turn-about.

"Will you... may I... can I see him?"

I took him in to be with his own son. He sat and held the left foot. Then, looking up at me, he asked if I could leave his son in the chapel of rest because he wanted to go home and bring in his wife so that she, too, could see her boy.

Following a "hit and run" incident a teenager died. The police asked me to provide her parents with support when they came to the chapel of rest to identify her. The Home Office pathologist had carried out a preliminary examination of her body and was waiting until her parents had identified her before he carried out the full post mortem examination. Her father was distraught.

"You can't let them cut her about any more. Hasn't she suffered enough already?"

The police sergeant glanced across at me as if to say "Now get your way out of that one!"[19]

I replied to the father "If she was my daughter I think I would feel exactly as you do. Does it help to think that, even at this stage, there may be something Tania can tell us about what happened, how it happened, and who caused it to happen? Would you want to give her that chance to tell us?"

With vehemence he replied "I would!"

They had produced a photograph of her. I explained that after the post mortem we would wash and brush her hair so that it looked just as it did in the photograph. Her mother said Tania was very particular about her hair, and mentioned the only shampoo she would use. I promised to try and get that shampoo and assured her that we would have her looking as lovely as we could when they brought her younger sister to see her later that day.

That evening they returned to the chapel of rest. Tania's hair was no longer matted with mud but washed, dried, brushed, and smelling of her shampoo. The police sergeant had telephoned me inviting me to pass on some information to Tania's parents. The post mortem had provided evidence which had led to the arrest of someone who had been charged with her murder.

---

19 *The coroner has an absolute discretion about whether or not, in such cases, there shall be a post mortem examination.*

Because it is so obvious I feel apologetic for stressing the point: "You cannot let go of that which you have been unable to grasp."

It is true physically.   It is also true emotionally and psychologically. It does not require that you touch the body, although, given the right support and constraints, this, as I have outlined, is often possible.

From time to time I am asked to advise families whether children should be "allowed" to see someone who has died. The general presupposition is that they should not do so, presumably because they might find it distressing. Maybe their grandparents remembered how, as children themselves, they had been compelled to touch a dead relative and had resented the compulsion. My experience of supporting children saying goodbye to dead brothers, sisters, fathers, or grandparents is that, without exception, they found it positive.

A twelve-year-old, accompanying her parents, brothers, and sisters to take leave of her three- month-old brother who had died, put a soft toy she had made for him in the Moses basket with him. She picked up a tissue and wiped first her mother's and then her father's eyes. She then took another tissue and wiped the eyes of the mortuary technician, and yet another with which to wipe mine. At the baby's funeral her five-year-old brother got up from his seat during my brief address, walked across to the little coffin, banged his hand on the lid, and asked "Is my baby brother in there?"

All I could do was stop in my tracks and reply "Yes!"

If Grandma has never hurt the children in her lifetime, why should they fear her now? To give them the freedom to see her, say what they want to say and take in that she is lying still, peaceful, and rested, is far less traumatic for them than to be told by clearly distressed parents that they must not see her. Their imaginations run riot. "Mummy and Daddy try to look after me and keep me safe. When they went to see Grandma after she had died they cried lots. If they won't let me see her it must be because she looks horrible—so horrible that it made them cry."

Rather than give a dogmatic "Yes. The children ought to see their sister/ grandmother/ etc." or "No. It's better that they remember her as she was;" I ask a question. "If it has helped you to see her and to take your leave, how are you going to explain to your children that, while it helped you, it won't help them?"

In my experience children can handle reality in a supportive environment much better than deception, which leaves them isolated and untrusting of all adults.

One boy put together his first sentence following his baby sister's death. "My Tammy's gone bye-byes." He then kissed her photograph. When his father came home from working a night shift he could see that his daddy was sad, and so he took his teddy bear up to his father's bedroom for him to cuddle in order to make him feel better.

Another told his friends that he hadn't got his sister any more and then listed her casually among the people he knew who liked to eat jelly.

I am told that below the age of seven most children lack the ability to comprehend the finality and irreversibility of death. This means that they are not burdened with the sense of an aching void which afflicts adults. Therefore the sight of someone dear to them who has died, so long as it happens in a supportive environment, is unlikely to be detrimental.

Many adults, having never seen someone who has died, are apprehensive when invited to take their leave of someone dear to them. A typical response to such an invitation is "No thank you. I'd rather remember him like he was." In cases where I suspect that this is a tactic to avoid the challenge, I offer to go and say goodbye on their behalf. It is surprising how enthusiastic people are in taking up this offer. When I return after, say, five minutes they look at me as if to see whether I have developed horns, a hunch back, or some other abnormality as a consequence of contact with the dead. Having determined that I am no different from the way I was beforehand they generally ask if I will take them to say goodbye. In my experience 19 out of 20 people who had been uncertain whether they wanted to see the body of a family member or friend subsequently told me they were glad they had. The other five per cent expressed no opinion.

Hospital staff and funeral directors are in an ideal position to help the bereaved with their conflicting emotions. Some people are embarrassed at having to admit that they have never seen a dead body. They have no idea how they will react to the experience. I admire the way some nurses handle grieving relatives. Typical is "I know that, whenever you were coming to see her, Mother insisted on wearing the bed jacket you had given her. We've put her in her favourite nightdress and the bed jacket. Her hair is brushed and, since she wouldn't receive visitors unless she was wearing her dentures, we've put them in ready for your visit."

Such attention to detail tells the family that Mother's welfare and comfort were important to the staff when she was alive, and that they have been no less diligent after her death. The fact that they have continued to care for her now that she has died seems to give permission for the family to overcome their diffidence and take up the invitation to see her.

Many members of staff, clinical as well as nursing, admit that they feel as if they have failed when their patient dies. Whether or not the death could have been avoided, or at least postponed, I try to get them to see that they still have a valuable role in the care of the bereaved family. If they can help them grasp the reality of the death at the time then they are engaging in good preventative medicine. As I shall explain later, people who were supported appropriately at the time of death make a significantly better adjustment to their bereavement than those who did not receive such support.

Bereavement first aid: Talking

Police officers often tell me that they feel bad at having to get statements from grieving families. My impression is that such people welcome every opportunity to recount their story, and thereby to help set it in context. Especially when a death has been sudden and traumatic it seems to help people to make sense of it, insofar as that is ever possible, if they can talk about the events surrounding it.   What Malcolm was wearing, what he had for breakfast before he set off on that fateful journey, how they heard on the local radio that there had been a pile-up, how they saw the police car pull up outside their house — minute details are rehearsed for every visitor who calls. Some journalists are ordered by their editors to "get a comment from the widow."   One or two reporters of my acquaintance have seen the importance for the family, not only of being able to rehearse their experience, but also of having a public acknowledgement of their private tragedy.

When Alex collapsed over the coffee table in his sitting room Nessie, his wife, sought my help. We lived not 50 yards away and she used to babysit for us. He had returned home from work and was eating his tea in front of the television. He was suspected by his G.P. of having a heart condition and was due to have tests the next day. For 25 minutes he laughed as he watched the Goodies, with Bill Oddie up to his neck in black pudding.[20] As the programme ended Alex keeled over and died. Nessie needed to have the enormity of this personal loss acknowledged. I encouraged her in her desire to write to the Goodies, thanking them for making her husband's last moments so happy. Graeme Garden replied in a handwritten letter that they were thankful she was able to look on their involvement so positively.

---

20 *Broadcast in March, 1975.*

After Alex's funeral Nessie agreed to be interviewed by a journalist whose integrity and sensitivity I trusted. The story of how he apparently died of laughter watching the Goodies appeared on the front page of most English Sunday papers. It was also reported in *World Medicine*. Talking to Hilary so that she could write up the story helped Nessie not only to get Alex's life, death, and memory, into context. It also helped her see that, at a national level, this was a significant event. If others thought Alex's dying was important she was entitled to feel it was a hundred times more important to her.

When our children wake at night, upset by a bad dream, we try to comfort them. Getting them to tell us what the dream was about sets boundaries around what is otherwise a limitless fantasy. The finding of words seems to scale down the terror. One child, who knew that she had a tumour growing inside her, was crying during the night. Her mother went to her and gently enquired why she was crying.

"I dreamt I went to sleep and didn't wake up."

"Then why are you crying?"

"I don't know" she replied, and went back to sleep.

Another youngster had leukaemia. Her parents were determined that, if they took her to Lourdes, she would get better. Upon her return home she was even more ill. I liked her and used to drop in on her most days. One afternoon she was lying on top of her bed fully clothed. The chemotherapy had caused her hair to fall out and so she wore a headscarf. Her wig lay discarded on her bedside locker, to be worn only when she visited the boys' end of the hospital ward. Her parents were sitting together on one side of her bed. Her eyes were closed and she lay with hands crossed over her chest. I stood at the other side of the bed and put my hand very gently on her right arm, so that if she was awake she would know that I was there, but if she was asleep I wouldn't disturb her. She opened her eyes, looked up at me, and smiled.

"I'm practising to see what it's like being dead!"

Her parents burst into tears and fled. She grinned as if to say "They can't hack it, poor dears!"

I told her that I was very impressed at how well she was practising. Later that evening her father said to me "When we took K. to Lourdes we demanded a miracle. We didn't get the miracle we asked for. What we have been given is an even greater miracle—that K. can face up to what is happening to her."

In this case it was a dying child whose direct talking cut through the pussyfooting round the subject. She restored realism to her relationship with her parents, and I had the privilege of hearing and watching it happen.

While ambulance paramedics are waiting for the arrival of a doctor or coroner's officer at a house where resuscitation efforts have been to no avail they are in an ideal position to encourage the bereaved relatives to talk. Not only are they likely to be given a full history of Father's "bronicals" or "farmer's lung", but they may well also be regaled with accounts of the escapades of his youth. I have even heard that photograph albums have been brought out to substantiate what a "catch" he had been 60 years ago for his now newly-widowed wife.

Talking clearly helped the injured young woman admitted to hospital after the death of her two little children, to whom I referred earlier.   The day after they died the doctor responsible for her care told me "If this woman survives it will owe more to you than to me."

This placed a heavy burden of responsibility on me, and I sought advice of the ward staff. They encouraged me in my proposal to offer to sit with her for up to half an hour each day, chatting if she wanted to or silent if that was preferable. The first explicit indication I had that my visits were welcome was when I received a telephone call from the ward one evening "R. wonders if you are coming to see her today."

Bereavement first aid: Tears

Why do we shed tears? "Alone among animals, man is the creature that weeps."[21] We may agree on the situations in which people are prone to cry—intense joy or sadness for instance. However, there is, as yet, no agreement as to what purpose, within the human body, tears serve. Nor has there ever been agreement as to their social acceptability. "Tears are good", runs one currently fashionable argument. They are a sign of humanity, softening and refining our perceptions of the world. They make us feel better. "Tears are bad", goes the other line of thought. They destroy the control of reason. Shedding them in public makes us vulnerable, something few people can afford in this harsh world. Above all, although forgiveable in women and children, they are highly suspect, not to say downright unworthy, when shed by men.[22] All tears are salty, but there are different sorts of tears. Reflex tears are triggered by, typically, the juice of onions. Emotional tears arise mainly from grief or joy. Even if the cranial nerve, which controls reflex tears, is severed, tears of emotion can still be shed. A biochemist, William H. Frey, and his colleagues collected, in test tubes, the lacrimations of hundreds of volunteers as they watched "tear-jerking" films.

He established that tears of emotion have a significantly higher protein content than reflex ones. So far as I am aware the precise nature and function of this protein emission has not been conclusively established, but it is widely agreed that the shedding of tears helps relieve stress. Frey wonders whether tears remove from the body toxic substances which build up as a result of stress.

---

21 *Curt Suplee, Smithsonian, Vol 15, No 3, June 1984.*

22 *Ibid. p.104.*

My own experience of the tears of emotion is that most of them end up in the stomach—"sniff, gulp, swallow." I am told that the concentration of salt (0.9%) is ideal for interacting with the acid generally present in the stomach. It provides the acid with something other than the lining of the stomach on which to work and to become neutralised. Furthermore such self-medication, or auto-pharmacology, unlike proprietary antacids, is free! When I ask students to describe how they feel after a good cry the responses include "worn out", "knackered", "empty". Apparently the shedding of tears of emotion triggers within the brain the production of endorphins. Not only do they sound like "morphine", they work like morphine, engendering a sense of peace, relaxation, and well-being. However, unlike morphine and other opiates, endorphins do not require two registered practitioners to draw up and administer them. They do not require an entry in the Dangerous Drugs Act Register. And they do not produce the undesirable side-effects of constipation and addiction associated with opiates. To cry when upset is to enable our bodies to provide us with the auto-pharmacology of nature's own poppy juice—and, like tears, it is free.

The notion that it is perceived as unprofessional for a doctor, nurse, chaplain, mortuary technician or any other health-care professional to find themselves moved to silent tears has, in my view, gone unchallenged for far too long. Of course it is reprehensible for any such member of staff to "milk the audience" for sympathy. That is an abuse of the patient or client for one's own self-gratification. But when the sorrow is genuine and the anguish of the client has touched an emotional nerve in the member of staff then I contend that there are several positive messages being conveyed to the client by our discreet tearfulness.

1. "Your own tears are not disproportionate. This tragedy, within my professional experience, justifies a tearful reaction."

2. "Not only did I care *for* your father [say], I cared *about* him."

3. "You may reasonably expect that I would have done my professional best to save his life (or make his dying comfortable and dignified), but in addition to my professional duty I had a personal agenda — the avoidance, if at all possible, of the pain I now feel at his death."

Without exception, in my experience, the reaction of bereaved relatives to the tearfulness of hospital staff has been positive.

Following the death of their child who had spent months in hospital the parents told the ward staff "You, all of you, are there to help, and can do things at times when we, who desperately want to do something, are helpless. You remove a great burden and give a great gift. So when someone dies, and you too are helpless, that sharing is the greatest gift anyone can want. I don't think the words you say matter at all. It's our feeling of sharing, of not having been left alone that matters."

The father of a young man did not want to be present when brain death was determined and the ventilator was turned off. He entrusted his son to the care of the staff nurse, Jo, who was assigned to him. We agreed that after death was confirmed I would ring the father to let him know. He had seen that Jo had been clearly upset as he took his leave of his son. I rang him and noted his response.

"I have been very touched at the way Jo dealt with us... She achieved the nice line between professionalism and compassion... Words can't express our appreciation of what you've done."

A woman whose husband collapsed in his armchair while she was preparing his birthday tea subsequently made contact with the Accident and Emergency Department where resuscitation was attempted without success.

"Death must be to you an everyday occurrence and yet you made me feel that this death, which meant everything to me, really mattered to you too, and you and all present showed to me the most sensitive sympathy and understanding. I cannot thank you enough."

A young woman recalled seven years after the death of her two-year-old what she had valued at the time.

"One of the sisters on the intensive care unit, and the way she helped me the most was, she sat and cried with me when M. died, and told me how much she cared about him. That helped so much — just to know that he wasn't a hospital number, that she really did care — enough to cry and share a grief with me..."

For one couple three pregnancies had ended either as late miscarriages or stillbirth. (A baby born dead before 24 weeks' gestation is classed as a miscarriage. One born dead after 24 weeks is defined as a stillbirth.) Their fourth child, Holly, survived for two hours. With such a medical history the woman was well known to the staff on the delivery unit. The tears of the staff helped her revise her view of life.

A month after Holly's death she wrote to me, and has given me permission to quote from her letter.

"Over many years now I have always taken any pain or sadness in my life as a punishment or very confusingly thinking it was because I was a bad person. When baby Mark died [five years earlier] it seemed so much so that I began to hate the world and everyone around as if they all believed too that I should have all this pain for punishment of all the wrong things I had done....

"The pain of losing Holly and not sharing in life with her in the years ahead is somehow different....

"It suddenly seemed as if everyone was sharing the pain. It was not punishment. It was Holly's life everyone was so sad for, they all wanted her to live. I somehow didn't feel guilty, didn't feel it was punishment. I can cry without guilty tears. I can miss Holly openly. I'm sure the staff around aren't aware of how much healing they are doing at such sad times....

"You do all make the pain easier, because you all care, thank you again for your kindness."

Subsequently the couple had healthy twin boys.

Some people seem to need permission to weep. Perhaps the alien territory of hospital, the unprecedented experience of bereavement, the staff with whom we are shy of expressing ourselves — any or all of these factors may conspire to make us feel as if we should maintain "a stiff upper lip". But when we detect even the slightest break in the voice of the nurse who brings us a cup of tea, it is as if she is letting us know that tears are legal tender.

Bereavement first aid: Tea

A famous antipodean singer was being interviewed on the radio. She was asked whether she had felt nervous before a much-publicised state occasion in which she had performed. With great dignity and in her beautiful classically-trained singer's voice she explained that it was "... then that I discovered that adrenalin is brown."

When shock sends adrenalin surging through our body there can be a number of reactions. Our mouth goes dry, our hands become clammy, beads of sweat develop on our top lip. Some people's stomachs churn so much that they are sick. Others, like the singer, need to relieve themselves. I am told that these are the responses to a primitive "fight or flight" instinct. The shock, whether of being chased by a bear or of being ambushed by the death of someone dear to us, results in a pounding heart beat and rapid breathing. Apparently oxygenated blood is directed to our muscles to facilitate running. The kidneys work overtime in removing spare fluid from the blood, resulting in our repeated visits to the lavatory. Once we have escaped from the bear we recover our breath, have a drink and a rest. After news of a death we have nowhere to run, no place of safety where the adrenal surge can be turned off. The kidneys, whose normal function, I gather, is to purge the blood of uric acid, are now running out of any more fluid to filter from the blood. As a consequence the uric acid stays in the blood and ends up circulating round the brain. This uraemic toxicity produces the kind of headache associated with hangovers.

The most obvious remedy for this dehydration is tea. In Britain it is widely accepted socially as a "pick-me-up" in stressful situations. Having made tea for the grieving family in the Relatives' Room in the Accident and Emergency Department I generally take additional mugs to the ambulance and police crews involved. They never refuse! Although many wards have a special china tea set for such occasions my own preference is for a mug. You can get both hands round a mug of tea, and if the stress has made them clammy the tea warms them up again. An anaesthetist friend has calculated that, in the first 24 hours after bereavement, the average weight adult needs to replenish up to four litres of fluid. That is the equivalent of one cup of tea per hour every hour. For those who do not drink tea, orange or other fruit juice may help restore the fluid balance. Alcohol may take the edge off the emotional pain, but it is a diuretic and can make the dehydration, and therefore the headache, even worse.

When I ask students whether they think about making their first cup of tea or coffee of the day most admit that they do not. It is so automatic—filling the kettle, turning it on, putting milk in the cup or mug, warming the teapot, adding the tea leaves or bag and boiling water—it is a routine requiring no conscious deliberation.

As soon as the police car is seen returning the bereaved family home the neighbourhood curtains begin to twitch. After a while the neighbours call to satisfy their curiosity and offer their condolences, enquiring if there is anything they can do to help. They are invited in and offered a cup of tea. I look on this simple act of hospitality as the beginning of the recovery process for the bereaved. They had been stunned, paralysed, immobilised by the news of a sudden death. Things were said to them. They were taken to identify the body. They were driven home. In all this they were the recipients of other people's direction. Now they are back at home they feel no less lost. Indeed the sight of Father's coat hanging by the front door, the armchair in which he dozed, the pillow on which his head will never rest again—all of these are reminders of the enormity of

what has just happened.   They could be excused for
standing, staring vacantly in catatonic shock.   But the
neighbours have called and so they make them some tea. By
doing so they begin to engage with the little routines of life.
They have been devastated but they are not incompetent.
Even if they cannot face the prospect of food, at least they
know how to make and take fluid.

Bereavement first aid: Time

When a man died on the operating table there was nowhere private for his wife to be with him. He was therefore transferred to a single bay in the intensive care unit which adjoined the theatre suite. He lay in a bed, just as if he was asleep. His wife sat next to him. After a while she said to me "I'm sure I can still see him breathing."

I replied "For the last 25 years when you have lain awake at night you have looked across at him. You have seen his chest moving as he breathed in his sleep. You can't rewrite 25 years' experience in 25 minutes. You need to allow yourself time."

For two hours we sat with her husband. We drank tea. She talked. She felt his hand becoming cool. She commented on the onset of rigor mortis. Then, quite suddenly she wiped away her tears and asked me if his corneae could be used for donation to other people. My answer was "Almost certainly." She had needed that two hours with her husband in order to take in the fact that he no longer required his corneae.

"I've told her he's dead" is one thing. "She has taken on board the intellectual, emotional, and personal implications of his death" is quite another. Allowing time, *at the time* of death, in order to make this transition, seems to save months of individual and family anguish later.

In that same intensive care unit young parents would sit and cuddle their children after they had died following attempts at corrective surgery. Their subsequent comments to me all pointed to the value of that time together immediately after the death. Typical are "I wasn't sure I wanted to see T. after her death but I am really pleased now that I did... We will never forget that night and the way you helped us with our grief;" "...Thank you for coming [25 miles through freezing fog to their home] on the night she died..."

I have described how, years later, on a neonatal intensive care unit, we gave parents the opportunity to cuddle, wash, and dress their babies after they had died. In the late 1970s and early 1980s this was all a bit radical. A grieving father asked for a photograph of him holding his newborn babe who had died after surgery, so that he could show the photograph to his wife who was in another hospital having given birth by Caesarian section. She had never seen her baby. The idea of taking and developing photographs of dead children caused raised eyebrows at the time. I think he was not joking when one member of staff enquired whether the camera would need to be autoclaved after such use!

In 1982 Professor John Emery of Sheffield University published research he had been carrying out into the deaths of babies aged between eight days and two years.[23] Any infant whose parents' place of residence at the time of death was in the area administered by the Sheffield Area Health Authority was included, even if the place of birth or site of death was outside the area. All 65 of such deaths between April 1979 and March 1981 were followed up. Obstetric records were studied, and, where they existed, so were paediatric and casualty notes.

Professor Emery visited most of the families about four weeks after the death. The rest were seen by the health visitor.   The home visits lasted about two hours and

23 *"Two year study of the causes of postperinatal deaths classified in terms of preventability." Archives of Disease in Childhood 1982, 57, pp668-673.*

involved not only the completion of an extensive questionnaire but also bereavement counselling.

I knew nothing of this research, nor even of the existence of John Emery, until he turned up in the hospital in which I was working in Leeds, asking to see me.

He laid out on a table seven sets of case notes and asked if I recognised any of the names. Not knowing the area in which he specialised I enquired how he came to be involved with these families. He explained the nature and purpose of his research project and how he had visited the families after their babies had died. Among other things he had been trying to assess how they were adjusting. Were the surviving siblings reverting to infantile behaviour as a means of seeking attention — temper tantrums, bed-wetting, underperformance at school? Were the fathers losing their will to work, losing their jobs, losing their sex drive? Were the mothers losing their ability to hold the family together, needing help from the G.P. or Social Services?

These families, he explained, pointing to the sets of notes, had all shown remarkably good levels of adjustment to their loss. And every set related to a family I had tried to support at the time of their baby's death. Because my name had featured in the families' accounts of their immediate post-bereavement care he had decided to make contact with me.

"What on earth are you doing?" he asked. "Because whatever it is we must get it replicated all round the country."

I described to him how we had encouraged the parents to have contact with their children after they had died. Some had wanted to help remove the tubes which had been supplying their medicines, and to wash and dress them. Some wanted to carry them to the chapel of rest. Some wanted to come back to the hospital once the death had been registered, bringing a coffin supplied by their local undertaker, so that they could take their little one back to Sheffield. If they wanted to talk to their babes or about them we encouraged them. We gave them "permission" to cry — often crying with them. We poured gallons of tea down their (and our) throats. And we gave them all the time they needed.

"Above all," John said, "You did it *at the time*."

I had been diffident in my account because I thought these were commonplace and obvious aids to parents in their grief. He described how, all too often, these techniques were invoked by bereavement counsellors months or even years after the death, when parents had already become dysfunctional because of unresolved bereavement. By "getting in on the ground floor" we forestalled these problems. He quoted one couple who had impressed him by their positive comments about the surgeon who had operated on their baby. Quite apart from their own desire that she should live, they wished she had survived in order to vindicate all the efforts the surgeon and the intensive care team had made on her account. Because they had already written to me in much the same vein I knew whom he was describing.

The sample may have been small — seven out of 65 — but John Emery assured me that it was statistically significant. Four weeks after the death of their infants these families were further along the road to the resolution of their bereavement than any of the others. He left me feeling not only encouraged that our "bereavement first aid" was effective, but also challenged as to how to get it disseminated and practised elsewhere. His evidence related to adults' grief following the death of a child. I saw no reason why the same principles should not also apply to adults mourning the death of adults. I already had evidence that being deprived of the opportunity to grasp the reality and irreversibility of the death of other adults who were dear to them had contributed to people being admitted to psychiatric units.

During the 1970s I was working in a hospital with some 800 psychiatric patients. At that time a large number of these people had spent many years in institutions and the hospital, with its spacious grounds, had become all they knew of home. However, among the acutely mentally ill I was struck by something quite a few had in common. Their lives had included bereavement. One patient's sister had been killed in a house fire. She had recurring vivid and frightening dreams of her sister with a black hole where her face should have been. Another woman had been discouraged from seeing or touching her stillborn baby. She was convinced that the whole episode of her delivery had been managed in order to remove her live baby from her care so that he could be looked after by someone else. One man was quite certain that his wife was dead, not because he saw her in the undertaker's chapel of rest (because he did not) but because he was convinced he heard her screaming as her coffin was rolled into the cremator. Others reported hearing "banging" from inside the coffins of their "dead" family members as their coffins were lowered into the graves. Yet others were convinced that their husbands or wives had "done a Reggie Perrin" — pretending to die in order to escape and lead a new life elsewhere with someone else.

As I listened to the patients describing their experience of bereavement I found a common theme. These people were "stuck" because they had been unable to "let go" of the person who had died. They said that they had not felt as if they were allowed to touch their relatives after they had died. My inference was that they had wanted to do so but had felt constrained by convention or prohibited by the authorities. They had been unable to grasp the reality of the death before the material evidence of that death was removed irrevocably from them by burial or cremation. This was especially significant in those cultures where it was customary for the burial to take place within a day of the death.

In another psychiatric unit the staff assumed that the number of Jewish patients as a proportion of the total number of patients roughly matched the proportion of the Jewish population in the hospital's catchment area. After I had raised the possibility that there might be a cultural reason for the patients being "stuck" in their bereavement the figures were looked at again. It was found that the proportion of Jewish patients was far higher than the local population would indicate. It was conceded that one of the likely contributory factors might well be that the patients had not been allowed time to grasp the reality of the death before the tangible evidence was buried.[24]

I was invited to make a presentation of my findings at a meeting of psychiatrists. My conversations with their patients hardly classed as formal medical research, and my conclusions lacked the statistical framework associated with such research.

When I described my findings and offered my impression that about one third of the acutely ill patients had, as a precipitating reason for admission as in-patients, an

---

24 *In hot climates before the days of refrigeration prompt burial was a practical, aesthetic, and hygienic necessity.*

experience of unresolved bereavement, I expected to be dismissed as an amateur. In the event the doctors suggested that I had probably *understated* the size of the problem. If there were 80 such bereaved people among a total of 800 in the psychiatric unit, then since, at the time, there were 70,000 such patients in hospitals across the country, a conservative estimate meant that there might be as many as 7,000 people, so broken by an unresolved bereavement that their mental health had become compromised to the extent that they needed in-patient care. One psychiatrist in particular saw the implications of this, and he urged me to look on good bereavement care as a form of preventative medicine.

I never had the opportunity to convey my own thanks to John Emery for his encouragement, nor to relay the thanks of countless families who have received the benefit of the bereavement first aid he insisted I replicated. John died on 1st May, 2000, trying to save his dog from a house fire. It was reported[25] that "...this was typical... he always put other people — even animals — before himself... he was a gentle and caring man."

---

25 *Daily Telegraph, Tuesday, 2 May, 2000. Quoted with permission.*

"The Birthday Boy"

When I first began work as chaplain to a large institution which was home to adults and children with learning difficulties I was warned about David. He was described as a "naughty boy", not least because he was inclined to wreck aerials and windscreen-wipers on cars, especially those on the car of my informant. When I first met David, whose age and height were obviously greater than those of a "boy", I took him to my car. I explained that it was nothing great, but it was all I could afford. I wondered whether he would look after it while I was at the hospital, making sure no one damaged it. His face lit up, he agreed enthusiastically, and my car never sustained damage at the hospital. It did, however, have its headlights kicked in and the windscreen wipers broken by some drunken revellers when it was parked outside a church while I was conducting a midnight service one Christmas Eve. My car and David had been safe within the hospital grounds, but not outside. He died after being knocked down by a car. It was a tragedy and a cruel irony.

The labels "mental handicap" or "people with learning difficulties", like most labels, often say more about the people who use them than about those they are describing. I discovered very quickly that a person whom others classify as mentally handicapped is by no means necessarily spiritually handicapped. Indeed, the absence of inhibition in self-expression frequently allows insights to find voice which can reduce the greatest academic theologian to silence.

Ronald was a free spirit who ambled nonchalantly around the hospital grounds. Just as I was clearing up one Sunday afternoon after a service in the large recreation hall he wandered in. I had taken the wooden crucifix down off the wall and was about to put it away when he elbowed me in the ribs.

"Oi!" he said. "Who's that?"

Holding the crucifix for him to see, I said "It's a special sort of picture of Jesus who loved us and died for us."

"Ugh!" he replied, and ambled off.

For a moment I stood still and thought "Lord, I did try!"

Then I continued on my way to the office where I put the cross away safely. Just as I was locking up the building Ronald hove in view again.

"Oi!" — another bruised rib. "But He's alive again!"

I like to think that there were smiles in Heaven at such a doctrinal jackpot.

On another Sunday we were midway through our "hymn sandwich" service when one person had a fit and crashed to the floor. Before any staff could reach her to help, Leonard who was nearby manoeuvred his wheelchair to get to her. He dropped to the floor on his paralysed and wasted legs, pulled the cushion out from the back of his wheelchair, and slipped it under her head. He even helped roll her over into the recovery position so that her head was on one side to ensure that she would not choke. There was no fuss, no "mercy dash" or "life-saving" heroics. He was familiar with what was done for people having epileptic fits and he simply got on with it. As I reflected with the staff afterwards "Who needs to teach them the parable of the Good Samaritan?"[26]

---

26 *Gospel of Luke, chapter 10, verses 30-37.*

Before my arrival at the hospital there had been a traditional carol service at Christmas. In that few members of staff attended I enquired whether the residents appreciated the format of nine lessons and carols. After all, few of them were familiar with shepherds and sheep, and there were no wise men at the hospital. The consultant in charge gave me a rueful smile at this assertion, but he agreed.

However, birthdays were a big thing. Everyone knew about them. Staff would help residents draw up an invitation list of friends whom they wanted to attend their celebration. On the day of a birthday the kitchens would supply a specially made birthday cake and there would be a party. On the Sundays before Christmas our services became something of a conspiracy to set up a party for Jesus's birthday. What sort of presents might He like? One resident turned up with a teddy bear, another brought a teapot. One who could not talk, brought a blanket. Another, who could talk, and did so at great length, suggested we gave him a present in the person of the prime minister of the time—Margaret Thatcher. The other residents seemed to think this was a reasonable idea, although members of staff were falling about with laughter. One person struggled in through the swing doors of the recreation hall, dragging a tea chest behind his wheelchair. In that tea chest he had placed a blanket, a hot water bottle, and a doll. Everyone crowded round Andrew's offering, and added their presents. They had created their own entirely unscripted nativity play.

On the Sunday before Christmas our "carol service" was a celebration of Jesus's birthday. The head chef wheeled into the hall an enormous cake he had made. Meanwhile the mighty Wurlitzer accompanied everyone singing "Happy Birthday, dear Jesus." The cake had been iced with a huge silver star and, just like other birthday cakes, had the name of the birthday boy on it. On the first such occasion I had been warned of the mess there was likely to be afterwards. I was not sure whether the domestic supervisor turned up out of curiosity or to threaten me with a broom if the place was left like a tip — or possibly like a stable. In the event we need not have worried. Not a scrap, not a crumb was left. It was like the miracle of the feeding of the 5,000,[27] except that there were only about 200 of us.

Each year thereafter the catering manager would check with me if "Jesus is having His birthday cake again?"

There are those who find this approach to the celebration of the Incarnation superficial, trivialising a profound event at the core of the Christian faith. It was after such a "birthday party" on Christmas Day one year that I had retired early and exhausted to bed. I was woken by my bleep. Nellie had died. Could I please come?

Nellie had been poorly for weeks. I think it was a humane decision to carry out her care in the terminal phase of her illness in her own bed, among her "family". The medical director of the local hospice had been visiting her daily to ensure that she was comfortable and free of symptoms. I drove through hail and snow and arrived, at midnight, at her bedside. The staff were standing or sitting silently beside her, and I knelt beside the bed and held her hand. We heard the shuffling of slippers and, in the subdued light, I noticed Ellen, who never missed a trick, coming in her dressing gown to join us. She knelt down beside me and explained to us all that "Nellie's spending Christmas with the Birthday Boy Himself!"

---

27 *Gospel of Luke, chapter 9, verses 12-17*

Amazing grace

Jock had fleas. He had been admitted to hospital and, with his customary generosity, had shared his fleas with the staff. Even Matron, the epitome of order and cleanliness, had been afflicted. It was expected of me at the time that when I visited in the hospital I wore a cassock, the black robe also worn for church services.

"Father Morris," she exclaimed. "Why is it that you're the only person not to have had a visitation from Jock's little folk?"

"Ah! Matron," I replied. "You see, they can't stand the smell of incense in my cassock."

"Oh! You dreadful man. You're having me on."

Jock recovered and was often to be seen in the park near the church. He would invite me to join him on the park seat and share his cider. I shared the seat but not the bottle on the grounds that his need of the cider was greater than mine. His was a gentle view of the world. He knew that some people considered him to be a blot on the landscape, but he meant them no harm.

One Sunday morning, as I arrived to unlock the church, I had to step over Jock who had crashed out in the porch at some stage during the previous night. If I tried to move him I would almost certainly have woken him up, and in any case, I asked myself, "Why shouldn't he sleep here?" The congregation began to arrive for the service. Some people expressed displeasure that a smelly tramp was in their way. The passage of scripture appointed to be read at the service was Jesus's story of the rich man who feasted sumptuously every day while, at his gate, lay a poor man, Lazarus, covered with sores. The poor man died and was carried away by the angels to be with Abraham. The rich man also died, and in Hades he saw Abraham far away with Lazarus at his side.[28]

I read the passage. The great organ played as the crucifer and acolytes returned to their places. I decided that the sermon I had prepared was not worth preaching, and so I did not climb up into the marble pulpit. Instead I stayed where I was and explained to the congregation that there would be no sermon. Since every one of us had stepped over Jock in order to get into the church, and since I was not certain that he was still alive, I suggested that we spend five minutes in silence, substituting "Jock" for "Lazarus", and reflecting on the response we would each make when challenged by our maker at the end of our lives. It was a long and uncomfortable five minutes. After the service the congregation could not get out fast enough. Jock was no longer in the porch. He had woken up and wandered off. Later in the week I sat with him and thanked him for being the best sermon I hadn't preached. Through his alcoholic haze he tried to make sense of what I had said, but at least he took it as a compliment.

Some years later, when I had moved to another church, I heard that Jock had died. Apparently some teenagers had given this harmless wayfarer a bottle of cider which they had spiked with Paraquat, a weed killer which, if ingested, destroys the liver. It had taken ten days to kill him.

Mother Teresa of Calcutta, describing her work in India with the poor,[29] said "They brought a man from the street, half eaten with maggots, and he said 'I've lived like an animal in

---

28 *Gospel of Luke, chapter 16, verses 19-31.*

29 *Sermon preached at Great St Mary's Church, Cambridge on 10 June, 1977.*

the street but I'm going to die like an angel, loved and cared for.' And he did die like an angel, he died a beautiful death."

Not many weeks later a tramp was admitted to our hospital in Leeds with a horrible fungating cancer. To start with he resented being in hospital. Indeed, I recall the ward sister describing him to me as a cantankerous old bugger. However, as we gained his confidence and eased his pain he mellowed.

I stood in the doorway of his room one morning when Sister and Staff Nurse went to give him some more analgesic. Sister sat on the bed beside him and put her arm round him so as to steady him while the staff nurse gave him an injection into his thigh. He looked up and said "Do you love me, Sister?"

"Yes, Jo," she replied. "We all love you very much."

"That's all right then," he said and drifted off to sleep, never to wake again in this life.

Harry had been brought into hospital from under a hedge. He was clearly not long for this life. I happened to be on the ward when he was warned how poorly he was, and so the staff asked me to keep him company for a while. He looked at me suspiciously and said "You're not a proper priest."

"That's all right," was my reply. "Would you like me to find out if Father Michael can come and see you?"

Grudgingly he agreed and so I went to ring my Roman Catholic colleague. While we were waiting for Michael Harry accepted my offer to stay with him "just as a friend."

A week later, on Easter Day, I was celebrating the Holy Communion on Harry's ward. Because Michael had been taken ill he was unable to bring Harry the Sacrament. I could see that Harry felt left out and so we gathered the other patients around his bed. Since the nursing officer wanted to make her Communion as well she joined us and (with his permission) sat on the edge of his bed. I explained that he was welcome to receive the Sacrament if he wanted to, but I would quite understand if he chose not to. When I had offered each person the bread and wine I came to Harry and gave him the cup and bread to hold for a moment, "to help you grasp that Christ has risen."

Having finished the service on that ward I moved to another. Later that evening the nursing officer caught up with me. Imitating his Irish brogue she said "Harry says you are a proper priest after all!"

Having completed all my scheduled duties one Christmas Day I called in at the home of a surgeon friend to leave a present for his family. He had been carrying out emergency surgery the previous night and was about to head back to the hospital to see how his patient was doing. I followed him across town. He came to a halt in the middle of a road junction above an urban motorway. When I saw a pair of legs sticking out from under the front offside of his car I stopped, put on my hazard lights, and ran forward, fearing that he had hit someone. In the event he had chanced upon an inert form lying in the road and had positioned his car so as to protect the body from other vehicles. He proceeded to check the pulse in neck, wrist, and, with no time for niceties over modesty, the groin. He felt for broken ribs, arms, legs, and was coming to the conclusion that the collapse was the spontaneous result of alcoholic over exuberance at the festive season when another car stopped. Two casualty officers, having just finished duty in Accident and

Emergency at a nearby hospital were on their way home. They provided second and third opinions which concurred. A passing taxi driver used his radio to summon an ambulance. The four of us were preparing to lift the "patient" so that we could move him out of harm's way when another car stopped and its driver shouted "Leave him alone! You'll kill him. Wait for a doctor!"

There are not many wayfarers who can lay claim to having received such prompt attention from a consultant surgeon and two senior registrars in Accident and Emergency at 1.10pm on Christmas Day. The ambulance duly arrived and took him to the detoxification unit. He may never have known what special attention he had received.

Monica was a regular visitor to our Accident and Emergency Department. Several times a week an ambulance would be called to the city centre because she had been beaten up or had hit the bottle. While drunk she was often abusive, but when sober she was perceptive, kind, and witty. When one of her fellow wayfarers died she asked specifically that I escort her to the chapel of rest so that she could say goodbye to him. It was as we were standing quietly beside him that she made me promise to take her funeral when the time came. She was so matter-of-fact about her poor prognosis that I felt humbled in her company.

Monica died, and I took her funeral. It was a very special send-off. Any number of her colleagues turned up, as did staff from Accident and Emergency. The person who ran the "caff" where she would often eat arrived just in time, still wearing her blue and white striped apron and check trousers. Several members of the ambulance service, acting on their own initiative, also attended. I asked them if they would like to carry Monica for her last time. They did. Her sixteen-year-old daughter volunteered to sing the first verse of "Amazing Grace" as a solo.   The rest of us had considerable difficulty clearing our throats to join in the second and subsequent verses.

I was reminded of Mother Teresa's story "I've lived like an animal in the street, but I'm going to die like an angel, loved and cared for." As we laid her worn-out body to rest I prayed, and still pray, that the angels carried Monica home safely.

Postscript

The season of Advent, as the word implies, is one of preparation for the coming of Jesus, not only as a baby at Christmas, but also as our judge. On the Saturday night before the first Sunday in Advent I was reading the passage from scripture appointed for the Sunday service.[30] In it Jesus is reported as describing how, at their day of judgement, the nations will be gathered before the judge. He will separate them, as a shepherd sorts the sheep from the goats. To those on the one hand he will say "Come, you that are blessed by my father .... for I was hungry and you gave me food, thirsty and you gave me something to drink, a stranger and you welcomed me, naked and you clothed me, sick and you took care of me, in prison and you visited me."

The righteous (Jesus's term, not theirs) reply "When did we see you hungry, thirsty, a stranger, naked, sick, or in prison?" The king will answer "Just as you did it to the least of these members of my family you did it to me."

It is difficult to put a time-scale on what happened as I reflected on this passage. I became aware, not of kneeling beside my bed, but of standing in the dock of a modern court. The high walls of the dock were solid, topped by a brass rail to which I clung. The only way out was down the steps to the cells below. Ahead of me, across the court, sat the judge in red robes. To my right sat the jury, and to my left was the prosecution counsel. He went through every minute detail of my life, casting everything I had ever said or done in the worst possible light. I tried to explain that "it wasn't like that" but was ordered by the clerk of the court to be silent.

---

30 *Gospel of Matthew, chapter 25, verses 31-46.*

Eventually the jury returned after deliberating. The foreman announced that they were agreed on their verdict.

"And what is your verdict?"

"Guilty."

I gasped, and it seemed as if that gasp echoed all round the court. I stood transfixed, clutching the rail and staring at the judge. He spoke slowly and deliberately.

"The verdict of this court is that you are guilty."

Then, in the slow motion of dreams, although I was awake, he stood up. He moved away from the throne, down through the well of the court, and came to stand outside the dock. With the words "... you are guilty" still ringing in my ears he continued "And the sentence is life."

As I stared, horrified, at him he grasped the rail and the whole side of the dock swung open. He reached in and took hold of my hand. Then, as he led me out, he added

"... Eternal Life."

Index

In the nature of this book the index is best used as a complement to the annotated contents list (which also functions as an abstract) on pages 5-6.